THE INDIANS
OF CALIFORNIA
✛

TIME® LIFE BOOKS

Other Publications:
JOURNEY THROUGH THE MIND AND BODY
WEIGHT WATCHERS ®SMART CHOICE RECIPE COLLECTION
TRUE CRIME
THE ART OF WOODWORKING
LOST CIVILIZATIONS
ECHOES OF GLORY
THE NEW FACE OF WAR
HOW THINGS WORK
WINGS OF WAR
CREATIVE EVERYDAY COOKING
COLLECTOR'S LIBRARY OF THE UNKNOWN
CLASSICS OF WORLD WAR II
TIME-LIFE LIBRARY OF CURIOUS AND UNUSUAL FACTS
AMERICAN COUNTRY
VOYAGE THROUGH THE UNIVERSE
THE THIRD REICH
THE TIME-LIFE GARDENER'S GUIDE
MYSTERIES OF THE UNKNOWN
TIME FRAME
FIX IT YOURSELF
FITNESS, HEALTH & NUTRITION
SUCCESSFUL PARENTING
HEALTHY HOME COOKING
UNDERSTANDING COMPUTERS
LIBRARY OF NATIONS
THE ENCHANTED WORLD
THE KODAK LIBRARY OF CREATIVE PHOTOGRAPHY
GREAT MEALS IN MINUTES
THE CIVIL WAR
PLANET EARTH
COLLECTOR'S LIBRARY OF THE CIVIL WAR
THE EPIC OF FLIGHT
THE GOOD COOK
WORLD WAR II
HOME REPAIR AND IMPROVEMENT
THE OLD WEST

*For information on and a full description of any of the Time-Life Books
series listed above, please call 1-800-621-7026 or write:*
Reader Information
Time-Life Customer Service
P.O. Box C-32068
Richmond, Virginia 23261-2068

This volume is one of a series that chronicles the history and culture of the Native Americans. Other books in the series include:

The Cover: A boy of central California's Nisenan people wears traditional emblems of prosperity and spirit power, including a headband fashioned of woodpecker feathers and a gorget made of abalone shell. When this picture was taken about 1870, the rich culture of the native Californians was being threatened by an onslaught of white immigrants.

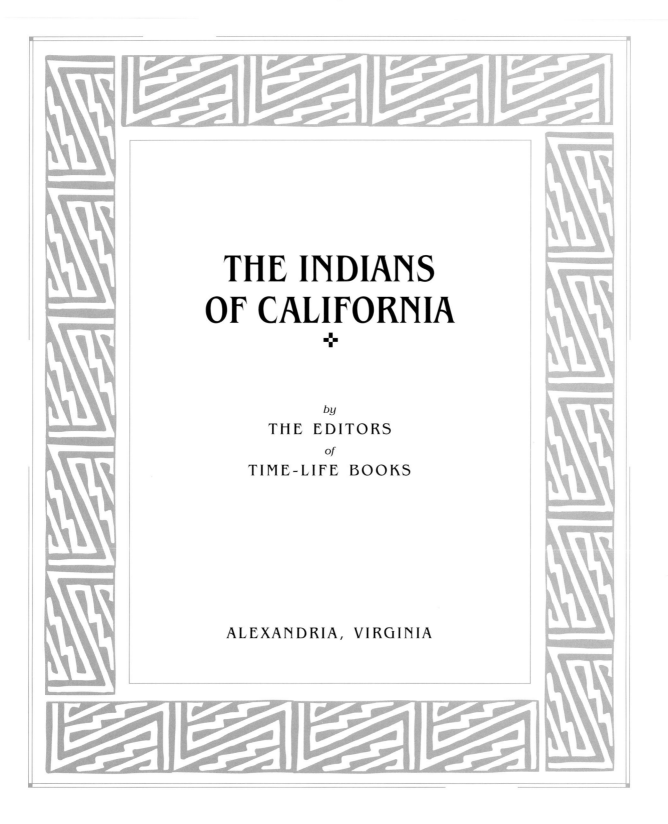

THE INDIANS OF CALIFORNIA

❖

by
THE EDITORS
of
TIME-LIFE BOOKS

ALEXANDRIA, VIRGINIA

Time-Life Books is a division of TIME LIFE INC.

PRESIDENT and CEO: John M. Fahey Jr.
EDITOR-IN-CHIEF: John L. Papanek

TIME-LIFE BOOKS

MANAGING EDITOR: Roberta Conlan

Executive Art Director: Ellen Robling
Director of Photography and Research:
John Conrad Weiser
Senior Editors: Russell B. Adams Jr., Dale M. Brown,
Janet Cave, Lee Hassig, Robert Somerville,
Henry Woodhead
Director of Technology: Eileen Bradley
Director of Editorial Operations: Prudence G. Harris
Library: Louise D. Forstall

PRESIDENT: John D. Hall

Vice President, Director of Marketing:
Nancy K. Jones
Vice President, New Product Development:
Neil Kagan
Vice President, Book Production: Marjann Caldwell
Production Manager: Marlene Zack

THE AMERICAN INDIANS

SERIES EDITOR: Henry Woodhead
Administrative Editor: Jane Edwin

Editorial Staff for *The Indians of California*
Senior Art Directors: Dale Pollekoff, Cynthia
Richardson (principal)
Picture Editor: Jane Coughran
Text Editor: Stephen G. Hyslop
Senior Writer: Stephanie Lewis
Associate Editors/Research-Writing: Mary Helena
McCarthy, Karen Monks, Robert H. Wooldridge Jr.
Assistant Editor/Research-Writing:
Annette Scarpitta
Assistant Art Director: Susan M. Gibas
Senior Copyeditors: Ann Lee Bruen (principal),
Anne Farr
Picture Coordinators: David Beard,
Betty H. Weatherley
Editorial Assistant: Gemma Villanueva

Special Contributors: George Constable, George G.
Daniels, Maggie Debelius, Marfé Ferguson Delano,
Thomas Lewis, Lydia Preston, David S. Thomson,
(text); Martha Lee Beckington, Barbara Fleming,
Christian Kinney, Kathy Wismar (research);
Barbara L. Klein (index).

Correspondents: Elisabeth Kraemer-Singh (Bonn),
Christine Hinze (London), Christina Lieberman
(New York), Maria Vincenza Aloisi (Paris), Ann
Natanson (Rome). Valuable assistance was also
provided by: Barbara Gevene Hertz (Copenhagen),
Trini Bandrés (Madrid), Constance Richards
(Moscow), Daniel Donnelly (New York).

General Consultants
Lee Davis is Assistant Professor of Anthropology
at the University of Nebraska. Dr. Davis is the author and editor of several publications, among
them "Locating the Live Museum," "Tracking Jede-
diah Smith through Hupa Territory," and *Going
Home: Returning Cultural Materials to Native California.* Her articles on the Maidu and Pomo Indians
have appeared in the *World Book Encyclopedia.*
Dr. Davis's extensive fieldwork in California Indian
communities has involved a collaboration with
more than 50 tribes. She has been a research fellow at the Newberry Library and has served on
several advisory committees at the National Museum of the American Indian in Washington, D.C.

Frederick E. Hoxie is director of the D'Arcy
McNickle Center for the History of the American
Indian at the Newberry Library in Chicago.
Dr. Hoxie is the author of *A Final Promise: The
Campaign to Assimilate the Indians 1880-1920* and
other works. He has served as a history consultant
to the Cheyenne River and Standing Rock Sioux
tribes, the Little Big Horn College archives, and
the Senate Select Committee on Indian Affairs. He
is a trustee of the National Museum of the American Indian in Washington, D.C.

Albert L. Hurtado is Associate Professor and Director of Graduate Studies in the Department of
History at Arizona State University. His research
and teaching interests include American Indian
history, the Hispanic and American Southwest,
and American frontier history. Dr. Hurtado is the
author of many publications, among them *Indian
Survival on the California Frontier.* He was awarded
the Ray A. Billington Prize for American Frontier
History in 1989 and has also been a recipient of
the Herbert Bolton Award in Spanish Borderlands
History. He is a historical consultant for the
Hoopa Valley Tribe.

Special Consultant
Lowell John Bean is Professor Emeritus of Anthro-
pology at California State University at Hayward.
He is a widely published author and editor whose
works include *California Indians Shamanism* and
*Mukat's People: The Cahuilla Indians of Southern
California.* Dr. Bean is also coauthor of *Temalpakh:
Cahuilla Knowledge and Uses of Plants, The Cahuilla
Landscape: The Santa Rosa and San Jacinto Mountains,* and coeditor of *Native Californians: A Theo-
retical Retrospective.* In his association with Cultural Systems Research in Menlo Park, Dr. Bean has
directed many ethnographical and archaeological
studies. He is a founder and member of the Board
of Trustees of the Malki Museum on the Morongo
Indian Reservation.

Library of Congress Cataloging in Publication Data
The Indians of California / by the editors of Time-
Life Books.
    p.   cm.—(The American Indians)
    Includes bibliographical references and index.
    ISBN 0-8094-9587-2
    I. Indians of North America—California.
    I. Time-Life Books. II. Series.
E78.C15I352 1994   94-4835
979.4'00497—dc20   CIP

CONTENTS

Majestic Mount Shasta has long been sacred to native peoples of the region, such as the Modoc and Achumawi, who occupied the plateau stretching eastward from the long-dormant volcano. Achumawis like the mother at right told their children of wondrous places on Mount Shasta, including a spring that harbored the tears of all deer, so that no deer would cry in anguish when it was taken by hunters seeking food or clothing.

A GIFT FROM THE SKY CHIEF

"Before there were people on the earth," begins a legend handed down by northern California's Modoc people, "the Chief of the Sky Spirits grew tired of his home in the Above World because the air was always brittle with an icy cold. So he carved a hole in the sky with a stone and pushed all the snow and ice down below until he made a great mound that reached from the earth almost to the sky. Today it is known as Mount Shasta."

Pleased with his accomplishment, the Sky Chief stepped from the clouds to Shasta's snowy peak and strode down its slope: "When he was about halfway to the valley below, he began to put his finger to the ground, here and there, here and there. Wherever his finger touched, a tree grew. The snow melted in his footsteps, and the water ran down in rivers."

As this tale illustrates, the Modoc, like other California Indians, recognized the handiwork of higher powers everywhere that they looked—in sculpted peaks and sunlit valleys, in murmuring rivers and silent glades. Their homeland was a fresh and vibrant place, where the potent beings that shaped the earth still touched the people and inspired them.

The Europeans who came to explore this bountiful region agreed that it was blessed. Spaniards dubbed it California, after an earthly paradise in a 16th century novel, and went on to colonize the territory in the name of their God and king. To native peoples, however, it was not one country but many. The lush rain forest of the northwest, the marshlands of the Central Valley, the wooded foothills of the Sierra Nevada, the shimmering beaches of the southern coast, the palm-shaded springs of the desert interior—each setting had its own demands and rewards and fostered a unique way of life.

What the diverse occupants of these distinct locales held in common was the belief that every life-sustaining creature and device came to them as a gift from the spirit world and that nothing in their environment should be taken for granted. As a Yuki holy man of the Mendocino woodlands explained as he led initiates around the rim of their tribal domain: "The rock did not come here by itself. This tree does not stand here of itself. There is one who made all this, who shows us everything."

A few miles inland from the northern California coast, lofty redwoods and firs line the banks of Redwood Creek, one of many swift-moving rivers that offered bounty to native villagers such as the Yurok fisherman below, shown lifting a long-handled dip net. Each year people prayed for the return of salmon, sturgeon, and steelhead trout, all of which surged upstream from the Pacific to lay their eggs, so crowding the waters that in the 19th century horses sometimes refused to ford streams during spawning season.

Clear Lake, nestled in the hills north of Santa Rosa where the Coast Ranges descend toward the Sacramento Valley, was a prized harvesting area for Pomo people such as the woman below gathering tule, a marsh grass used to make homes, watercraft, and household implements. Before runoff from the Coast Ranges and the Sierra Nevada was diverted to cities and farms, large areas of central California were covered with wetlands resembling this tranquil basin—home to abundant waterfowl, celebrated by some tribes as among the first creatures on earth.

Oak trees and outcroppings of bedrock stud the western foothills of the Sierra Nevada. Both were used by people like the Foothill Yokuts woman below, shown grinding acorns into meal in a bedrock mortar under the shade of bent saplings. Many California Indians looked to oak trees for sustenance and greeted the autumn acorn harvest with dances and songs.

Waves fetch up against the Pacific coastline below Morro Bay, an area that was once the domain of the Chumash, a large and prosperous tribe devastated by contact with Europeans. As shown below by a Chumash named Fernando Librado, who survived to document the traditions of his people, members of the tribe strung together disk-shaped shell beads and used them as currency. Many other rewards came to the people from the sea—including beached whales, which the Chumash believed were driven ashore by spirits who dwelt beneath the waves.

A grove of fan palm trees offers welcome shade amid the desert terrain of the Cahuilla, near the oasis known today as Palm Springs. Carrying coiled burden baskets like the one balanced by the Cahuilla woman below, the desert dwellers harvested dates from palms and scores of other fruits, seeds, pods, roots, and tubers found throughout their domain. "Nature did not pour out her gifts lavishly here," observed a visitor to Cahuilla country in the late 1800s, "but the patient toiler and wise seeker she rewarded well."

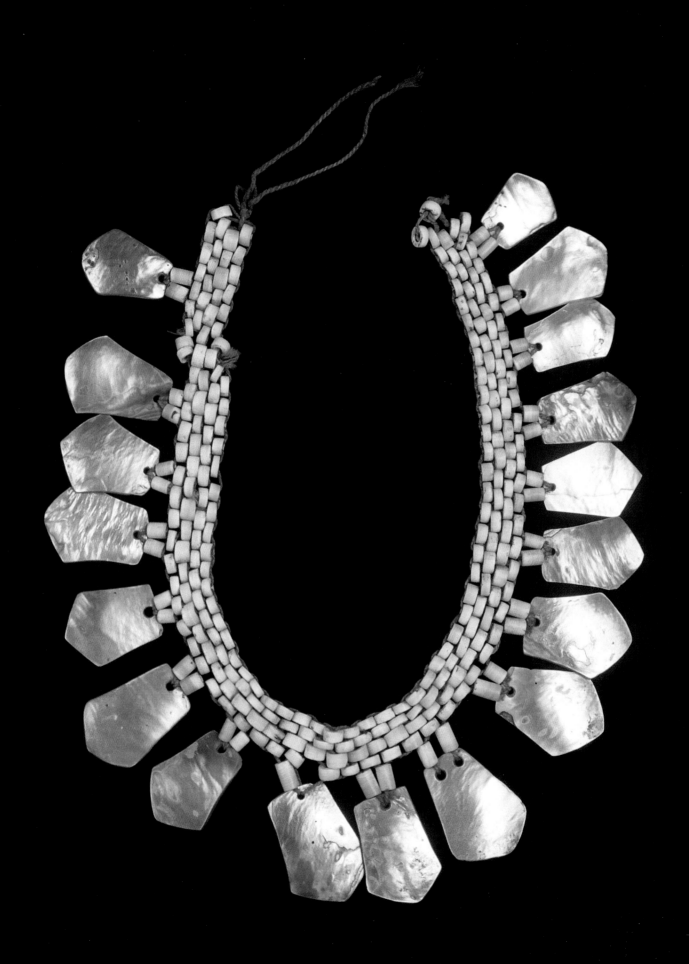

1

DWELLERS IN A LAND OF PLENTY

Glistening pendants carved from abalone shells hang from a band of disk-shaped clamshell beads in a necklace made in central California. Acquired by a Russian traveler in the early 1800s, the necklace is counted among the earliest artifacts of California Indian culture.

On a crisp December afternoon in 1991, four elderly Monache Indian women met with representatives of the U.S. Forest Service in a woodland at the western edge of the Sierra Nevada, near Shaver Springs, California. They assembled in a large clearing crowded with tall, thickly bunched clusters of deer grass. Soaproot, wild sunflowers, and sourberry shrubs grew along the fringes of the clearing. The old women knew this vegetation well. For thousands of years, such plants had flourished in the Sierra foothills, sustaining the Monache people by providing them with food, medicine, and the raw materials for their baskets, cordage, clothes, and shelters. But the women recognized sadly that no one would reap much benefit from these poor specimens.

Sisters Martha, Lydia, Edith, and Melba Beecher cast a practiced eye over the ragged growth. The ground beneath the trees was crowded with bear clover, a pesky shrub nicknamed "mountain misery." Scrubby incense cedar and ponderosa pine crowded the stately oaks, pushing up into their leafy canopies; few acorns would grow on those branches. The sunflowers were infested with insects, harbingers of a poor summer seed harvest. And the twisted sourberry branches would yield scarcely a dozen of the 500 or more straight sticks needed to fashion a cradleboard.

Melba Beecher prodded gently at one of the slender deer-grass flower stalks of the kind she and her sisters, like their mother before them, gathered to weave baskets. As many as 3,750 such stalks went into a medium-sized Monache cooking basket. Properly tended, a healthy plant might produce 75 stalks or more. But few of these plants had more than a brittle handful apiece. Each cluster appeared to be suffocating in old growth that stifled all but the hardiest of infant shoots. "They'll die," said Martha Beecher. The others agreed with her: "They'll have to be burned."

For the Beechers knew well what modern-day naturalists were just beginning to learn: that before white people came, the Indians of California had used fire as an environment-shaping, life-sustaining tool. The women's ancestors would have long since set ablaze the old deer grass and the matted underbrush of the surrounding forest to allow fresh growth to flourish. Controlled burning opened forage areas for wildlife, returned nutrients to the soil, and eliminated weeds and pests along with withered plants and grasses that provided tinder for wildfires. Thanks to such precautions, the first Californians were seldom threatened by infernos of the sort that ravaged the hills above Oakland in 1991 and blackened the skies around Los Angeles in 1993.

But controlled burning had long been discouraged in California by authorities who regarded the practice as wantonly destructive; edicts against burning dated back 200 years to the early days of Spanish colonization. Only recently had ecologists and foresters begun to appreciate the rejuvenating role that fire plays in the natural cycle. The little group gathered outside Shaver Springs that afternoon in 1991 was participating in a pilot project aimed at maintaining native plants for traditional crafts such as basket weaving. Kat Anderson, an ethnobotanist studying the use of wild plants by indigenous peoples, had selected this site and persuaded the Forest Service to try the burn. She was present that day—and would return over the following months—to study the effects of the fire.

As the others watched, a forest ranger stepped forward and set fire to one of the large deer-grass clusters. Fanned by a light westerly breeze, the flames quickly spread to other clumps, filling the air with greenish smoke. "They look happy," Martha Beecher said softly of the crackling grasses. "Next year you can burn that," she added, pointing out the gnarled sourberry to a member of the fire crew.

Martha Beecher knew that burning would clear the way for healthier vegetation to emerge—and time would prove her right. As flames consumed the old growth, she and her sisters had tears in their eyes. "They told me later that they were thinking about their ancestors," recalled Anderson. "They knew that their ancestors were smiling."

Although the original Californians were dismissed by European intruders as primitive hunter-gatherers and long excluded from any role in managing the land, they shaped the environment with great ingenuity, improving their prospects by burning, pruning, sowing, weeding, irrigating, tilling, and harvesting. These age-old practices—evolved through trial and error and sustained by faith and folklore—reflected sound ecological principles. The region's first inhabitants did not plow fields and plant crops, but they worked the land intently. Native California, popularly regarded as a wilderness inhabited by simple foragers, could be more accurately characterized

The tribal territories outlined on the map at right only suggest the astonishing diversity of California's once-large native population—about 300,000 when the first Spaniards arrived on the scene in 1542. The majority of these tribal designations refer to groups sharing a common heritage and speaking languages derived from a common stock. Each group was fragmented into smaller tribal communities, however—more than 500 in all—that were separated from one another by the natural boundaries of California's endlessly varied topography.

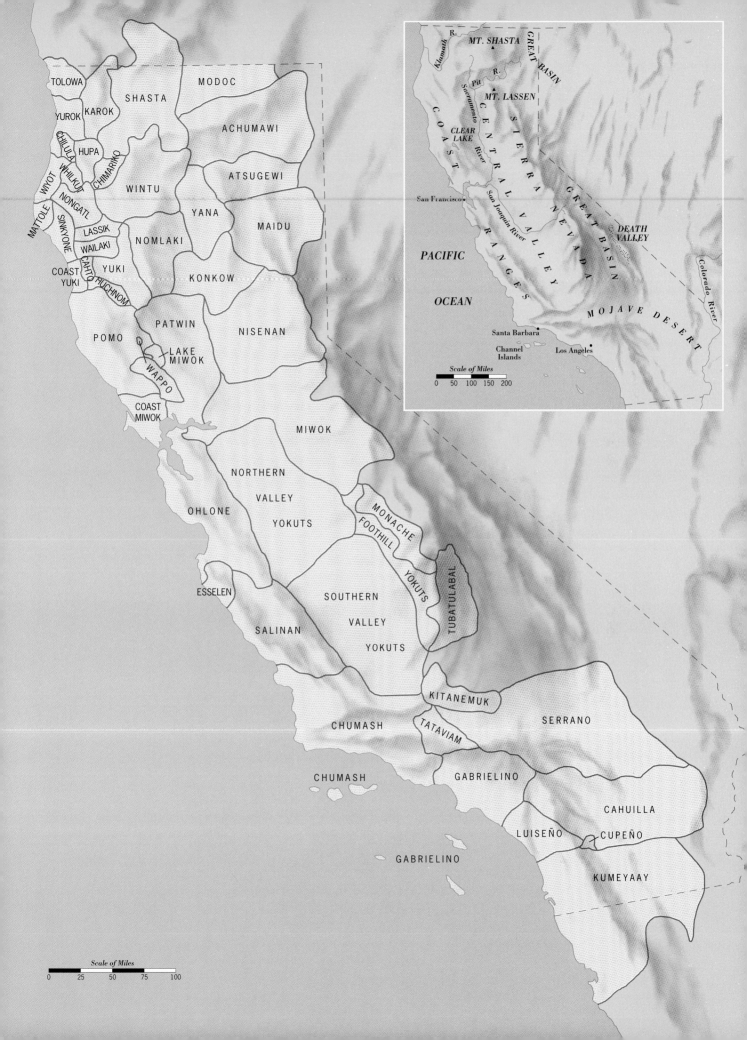

TOLOWA

YUROK

KAROK

SHASTA

MODOC

CHILULA

HUPA

CHIMARIKO

WHILKUT

WIYOT

NONGATL

WINTU

ACHUMAWI

ATSUGEWI

MATTOLE

SINKYONE

LASSIK

YANA

WAILAKI

NOMLAKI

MAIDU

COAST
YUKI

CAHTO

YUKI

HUCHNOM

KONKOW

POMO

PATWIN

LAKE
MIWOK

NISENAN

WAPPO

COAST
MIWOK

MIWOK

OHLONE

NORTHERN

VALLEY

YOKUTS

MONACHE

FOOTHILL

YOKUTS

ESSELEN

SOUTHERN

VALLEY

YOKUTS

TUBATULABAL

SALINAN

KITANEMUK

CHUMASH

TATAVIAM

SERRANO

CHUMASH

GABRIELINO

CAHUILLA

LUISEÑO

CUPEÑO

GABRIELINO

KUMEYAAY

Klamath R.

MT. SHASTA

GREAT BASIN

Pit R.

Sacramento

MT. LASSEN

CLEAR
LAKE

Sacramento River

COAST

San Francisco

San Joaquin River

SIERRA NEVADA

CENTRAL VALLEY

GREAT BASIN

DEATH
VALLEY

PACIFIC

RANGES

Colorado River

OCEAN

MOJAVE DESERT

Santa Barbara

Channel
Islands

Los Angeles

Scale of Miles

0   50   100 150 200

Scale of Miles

0   25   50   75   100

as a vast and skillfully tended garden. Such was its bounty that it supported one of the highest concentrations of people north of Mexico. At the time of initial European contact, just 50 years after Columbus's first voyage across the Atlantic, the land that now constitutes the state of California had a population of some 300,000.

The inhabitants of this region enjoyed the most varied diet on the continent. People in other areas relied heavily on a single staple such as corn, salmon, or buffalo. If that resource grew scarce, entire communities went hungry. The first Californians were not always free from want, but nearly every village had access to at least three staples: fish, deer, and acorns, from which the Indians derived a nutritious flour. And the mild climate and fertile soil, the long coastline, and the teeming forests and waterways supported an astonishing array of additional resources. If the oaks failed to bear or the fish did not run, there were some 500 other plants and animals to fall back on—an opulence that enchanted visitors from more stringent environments.

Europeans likened this generous land to Eden and filled their diaries and ships' logs with descriptions of its prodigious allure. California was a land of "inexpressible fertility," declared French explorer Jean-François Galaup de La Pérouse, who sailed into Monterey Bay in 1786. "There is not a country in the world which more abounds in fish and game of every description," he wrote. Other immigrants were transported by the towering redwood forests, the "vineyards" of wild grapes, the lush meadowlands, and the verdant fields and hillsides that seemed to have been landscaped by nature's hand, like an "English park," in the words of one diarist. Even the gold-rush adventurers who inundated California after Mexico ceded the territory to the United States in 1848 paused long enough in their frenzied quest for riches to scribble letters home expressing awe at the fragrant fields of pink, purple, yellow, and white wild hyacinths that graced the hills around their mines.

But while all of the newcomers admired the land, they generally held its residents in low regard. California's Indians had built no imperial cities or stone temples. Separated from competing populations by formidable natural barriers of mountain and desert and well provided for by their surroundings, they had little reason to forge alliances or vie for territory. In European eyes, these peaceful, lightly clothed people with few possessions seemed inferior to America's other Indians—to the wealthy Aztec or the assertive Iroquois, to the industrious Pueblos or the charismatic Plains horsemen. Observing how they pried roots and bulbs from the soil with pointed sticks, the goldminers contemptuously labeled them Diggers.

Outsiders persistently failed to recognize the extent to which the native Californians studied the land and coaxed forth its blessings. In early summer, tribes living in regions along the southern coast and in the foothills of the Central Valley harvested a now-extinct grass that bore a small grain about half the size of wheat. After each harvest, they burned the fields and scattered some of the grain, mixed with the seeds of other annual plants, over the ash-covered soil. The Spaniards wrote glowingly of the lush "natural pastures" that resulted but ignored the contribution of the Indians. Father Gerónimo Boscana, a Spanish missionary of the early 19th century, wrote of an area blanketed by such grasslands that "in no part of the province was to be found aught but the common, spontaneous productions of the earth."

The false assumption that the original Californians were artless and indolent provided outsiders with a rationale for imposing on them and exploiting their resources. Spanish friars confined tens of thousands of Indians to missions in an effort to convert them to Christianity and make them more productive, but the tragic effect of the mission system was to disrupt time-honored subsistence patterns, expose Indians to the ravages of European-borne diseases, and leave the survivors at the mercy of settlers who cared little for their welfare. Many of the enterprising newcomers who flocked to the state in the 1800s as the missions declined regarded the indigenous peoples as property, to be used up and discarded—or as pests, to be driven away or exterminated. California, the land of promise, became the setting for some of the saddest episodes of abuse in the sorry history of white-Indian relations.

Those traumatic times left scars both on the Indians who endured and on the countryside they cherished. Among the natural assets imperiled by the gold rush were the wild hyacinths that so impressed the forty-niners. It was the Indians themselves—the lowly Diggers—who kept the hills carpeted with those blossoms, which grew from small round bulbs called brodiaea that were cooked and eaten like miniature baked potatoes by native peoples in many parts of the state. To ensure an ample yearly supply, young girls were taught from an early age to carefully subdivide brodiaea, taking only the large "mother" bulbs and replanting their offspring—clusters of as many as 50 tiny bulblets the size of a baby's fingernail. Returning repeatedly to the same gathering spot, loosening and aerating the soil with their sharp digging sticks, these hardworking gardeners kept the hyacinth in lavish bloom year after year. But within a generation of the forty-

This regalia was likely made in central California in the early 1800s and worn by men in ceremonial dances. It includes, from top to bottom, a topknot of magpie tail feathers, another of brown pelican wing feathers, and a boa of trimmed waterfowl feathers.

niners' arrival, most of the women were gone—driven off, enslaved, felled by disease, or murdered by callous intruders. When the women came no longer, their flowers disappeared.

The intruders and their technology had other drastic effects on the native environment. Through feverish activity, the new Californians reaped phenomenal returns from the land, but some resources were exhausted in the process and others were endangered. Grazing and overhunting left vast areas virtually devoid of game; runoff from farms and mining sites fouled the streams where fish spawned; water-diversion projects dried up marshlands and depleted fowl and forage. Indians in most parts of the state were left with little choice but to abandon their traditional methods of subsistence.

But like a field swept by fire, the indigenous culture of California harbored the seeds of renewal. Indian communities persisted in locations that whites considered too arid or remote to covet for development. There, the customs of the elders were perpetuated by the young. And in time, Californians of European ancestry began to ponder the uncertain future of their natural inheritance and listen to the people who had the longest ties to this generous but fragile land. What they heard were words of caution and hope. As Mabel McKay, a 20th-century Pomo healer and basketworker, put it, gifts like the wild hyacinth and its nutritious bulbs were made to be taken, but taken with care. "When people don't use the plants, they get scarce," she observed. "You must use them so they will come up again. All plants are like that. If they're not gathered from, or talked to, or cared about, they'll die."

The same philosophy applied to wildlife, which was appealed to in respectful terms and culled in painstaking ways that reduced the risk of depletion. Through such methods, native Californians have impressed on newcomers the need for partaking wisely of the land's bounty so that the rewards will last not just for decades or for centuries but for generations beyond number. In the words of Kathleen Rose Smith, a Californian of Pomo and Miwok ancestry, "To live in spiritual and physical balance in the same small area for thousands of years without feeling the need to go somewhere else, as my people did, requires restraint, respect, and knowledge of the ways of each animal and plant." Such keen regard for nature, she added, stems from an abiding sense of kinship: "As my mother taught me, and she, in turn, was taught, the plants, animals, birds—everything on this earth—they are our relatives, and we had better know how to act around them, or they'll get after us."

A cloak made from the skin and feathers of a single California condor envelops the wearer within the giant bird's 9-foot-8-inch wingspan. Many tribes danced to honor the condor, revered for its ability to communicate with the supernatural world.

The cloak shown below, made of glossy raven feathers on a net base, was worn by a dancer impersonating a powerful spirit in annual rituals of the Nisenan and Miwok to ensure prosperity and health.

California is young in geologic terms, its recent origins in volcano, earthquake, and glacial ice still evident in its chiseled topography and dramatic physical diversity. Among the natural barriers that long impeded movement and set one tribe apart from another are two mountain chains— the fog-swept Coast Ranges and the snowcapped Sierras. Between the two lies the Central Valley, a fertile drainage basin that extends southward from the vicinity of Mount Shasta for more than 400 miles before yielding to parched hills and desolate salt flats. Although generally mild, the climate of California embraces the continent's broadest extremes, from the bone-chilling, subzero winters of the Sierras and the northeast plateau to the scorching summers of the southern interior. The redwood forests of the northwest coast are among America's wettest regions, while the deserts at the lower end of the state are among the driest.

No one knows when humans first came to California. The archaeological record suggests that they began arriving more than 10,000 years ago, as the Ice Age waned. Migrating bands of hunters, whose Asian ancestors had crossed the Bering Strait from Siberia into Alaska centuries earlier, found a bounty in the herds of mammoth, bison, sloth, and other large herbivores that browsed beside the huge freshwater lakes then covering much of interior California.

In ancient times as in recent centuries, this land of plenty attracted a remarkable assortment of peoples. The early Californians belonged to at least six major language families, whose other members fanned out across the length and breadth of the continent. Among the first to arrive were Hokan speakers, related to Yuman tribes such as the Quechan and Yavapai of present-day Arizona; the Hokan speakers found homes in the far south as well as in pockets of central and northern California. A smaller group, the Yukian speakers, whose descendants settled in the forests of today's Mendocino County, may have arrived about the same time. Penutian speakers, linguistic cousins of New Mexico's Zuni, swept in on the next great migratory wave and came to dominate the Central Valley. They were followed by Algonquian speakers in the north and Uto-Aztecan speakers in the south—members, respectively, of language families that spread east to the Atlantic and south deep into Mexico. Last to reach the area were Athapaskan speakers, relative latecomers to the New World, some of whom migrated down from the Far North to establish villages in northwestern California.

There were apparently no large-scale population incursions after about AD 1300. By then the climate had long since warmed, and the glaciers had retreated. The big lakes had evaporated, leaving behind the salt marshes and dry beds of Death Valley, Mono Lake, the Salton Trough, and the Mojave Desert. The herds of big game had died out as the lush lakeside vegetation withered, and the hunter-gatherers had put down roots. Once they were settled, individual bands tended to stay in one place, adapting their tools and technology to the varied, small-scale foraging opportunities of their local environments.

The relative isolation of peoples transformed an already diverse region into a linguistic crazy quilt. In the northwest, for example, the Athapaskan-speaking Hupa settled near the Algonquian-speaking Yurok and the Hokan-speaking Karok. Over time the three groups interacted and developed similar customs, but their languages remained worlds apart. Elsewhere neighboring groups with common origins evolved distinct tongues. In one case, a band of Yana Indians near Mount Lassen took the process further by developing different ways of speaking for men and women. Fortunately the two sexes could understand each other's idiom.

By the time Europeans made contact, the six original families had spawned upward of 90 languages, which in turn had fragmented into a welter of dialects—more than 300 in all, according to one estimate. "The diversity of language is so great in California," wrote Father Boscana, "that almost every 15 or 20 leagues you find a distinct dialect so different, that in no way does it resemble the other." More than 100 tribes resided in the area bounded by the present state borders. Most were in fact tribal groups, consisting of numerous bands that spoke related dialects; those bands

SHELTERS FOR A DIVERSE LANDSCAPE

"From the outside, at a distance, the whole thing was hardly visible," recalled a visitor to an Achumawi pit house in the 1920s. "It was just a large mound of earth with grass growing over it except that you might notice a plume of smoke coming out of it, and the ladder sticking out. You walked to the top, and peered down the hatchway, and it was like looking down into a cavern. You saw the fire, and then you could make out the shapes of people."

This was one of the distinctive dwelling types built by the early inhabitants of California—a lodge framed in timber over an excavated pit and covered with an insulating layer of earth. From the plateau country of the Achumawi and Modoc in the northeast to the hills and valleys of the Pomo, Patwin, Miwok, and their neighbors in central California, pit houses were favored as winter shelters. And in many parts of California, people built similar structures with excavated floors and banked-earth exteriors as sweat houses or assembly lodges.

Otherwise, the region's housing varied widely, depending on the climate and the available resources. In the northwest, the Yurok, Hupa, Karok, and others took advantage of the lofty redwoods and cedars to construct gabled plank houses. Other groups living in forested areas erected conical, tipilike lodges of poles covered with bark, such as the one shown below. People in warmer settings frequently put up lightweight structures thatched with branches, reeds, or grass. Even within the territory occupied by a single tribal group, there were subtle variations from place to place, dictated by local circumstances and customs.

Strips of bark provide the sheathing for this Monache house, framed of pine poles lashed to a forked center post. The Monache peoples, who lived at elevations of several thousand feet along the western slopes of the Sierras, often insulated such conical lodges with earth, banked up around the wall.

An elderly basket maker sits in the doorway of her house, a reed-and-brush structure of the sort common in Indian villages of the southern California desert. An attached ramada provides a shady working area.

Photographed at the turn of the 20th century in Atsugewi territory in northeastern California, this "tcimaha," or sweat house, is layered with bark slabs. Whether framed of wood, earth, or brush, tribal sweat houses were cherished gathering places for men.

A horizontal ridgepole supported by a pair of forked end posts forms the spine of this house belonging to a Southern Valley Yokuts family. The walls consist of tule mats tied to a framework made of bent saplings.

Located along the upper Fresno River at the eastern edge of California's Central Valley, this brush house, which was thatched with leafy branches, was built by the Chukchansi, one of the Foothill Yokuts bands.

Religious and social life among many central California tribes centered in communal earth lodges such as this Pomo assembly council chamber. The largest of these structures were earth-covered dance houses built over excavated pits up to 60 feet in diameter.

This 1920 Hupa dwelling typifies the cedar and redwood structures found in northwestern California's forested river valleys. The design was similar to that of the Yurok houses described by a Spaniard in 1775 as "well constructed of thick planks, with circular entrances barely the width of a human body."

were in turn made up of a few to as many as a dozen or more villages whose inhabitants shared a well-defined territory and were guided by a single chief or a council of leaders.

The bands within a single tribal group sometimes occupied quite different settings and generally saw little of each other except when parties came together to trade or take part in a ceremony that reflected their common cultural heritage. The people known collectively as Pomo, for example, were spread out across most of what is now Sonoma, Lake, and southern Mendocino Counties: Some lived by the Pacific; some made homes along the rivers feeding into the sea; and others resided on the far side of the coastal range in the vicinity of Clear Lake and nearby streams flowing down toward the Central Valley. All told, there were 34 autonomous Pomo bands, whose Hokan-derived dialects were as different from one another as English, German, and Dutch. Here as among other diffuse tribal groups in California, each band spoke for itself.

Few of the large tribal groups even called themselves by a single name; such designations were most often bestowed by outsiders. The Yukian-speaking people of northern Mendocino County, for example, named themselves after their surroundings—Ukoht-ontilka, or "beside the big water," for coast dwellers; Huchnom, or "tribe outside the valley," for those who lived in the rugged country along the South Eel River. Their collective name, Yuki, was applied to them by a nearby Wintu band and meant "stranger" or "enemy." Many groups received their enduring tribal names from the Spaniards. The Chumash of the south-central coast and the Channel Islands, for example, took that title from a Spanish corruption of *mitcumac* or *tcumac:* terms that were used by coastal peoples to describe the occupants of Santa Cruz and Santa Rosa Islands. In other instances, Spanish tribal names owed nothing to the native language and referred instead to the mission with which certain Indians were associated, such as the Luiseño of the Mission San Luis Rey or the Gabrielino of the Mission San Gabriel, or to their locale—Serrano for mountain people, or Costanoan for coast dwellers.

Much as outsiders imposed arbitrary titles on the Indians, they defined California in a way that had little to do with native settlement patterns. The Spaniards and later intruders saw the lower Colorado River as an obvious dividing line,

These small Chumash animal effigies were carved from soft soapstone and polished to a high black gloss with grease and soot. Whales, like the example below, were popular subjects for such carvings because the Indians believed they herded seals to shore for the benefit of the hunter; the stylized pelican (above) may have been a fishing talisman.

and the river became the southeastern border of the state. Yet both banks of the lower Colorado were home to tribes such as the Mohave and Quechan who cultivated corn and other crops and had more in common with the pueblo dwellers to their east than with the Indians to their west. The significant barrier was not the Colorado but the forbidding desert that separated the river dwellers from the resourceful foragers of southwestern California, whose arid environment was relieved by springs and seasonal streams. Similarly, American officials in the 19th century drew up a boundary with Nevada that included in California portions of the Great Basin—home to the Paiute, the Shoshone, and other nomadic peoples who had little affinity with the settled tribes living west of the Sierras. For the early Californians, those rugged peaks and the severe desert at the lower end of the range marked the eastern frontier of their fruitful domain.

Within this broad geographical framework, there were various ecological zones that called for different subsistence strategies. Perhaps the most de-

A finely woven basket, probably made in the early 1800s by an Ohlone or Coast Miwok woman to present as a gift, is decorated with Olivella shell beads that have been strung on the sedge-root sewing strands. Collected by coastal tribes, Olivella shells were widely traded as currency throughout California.

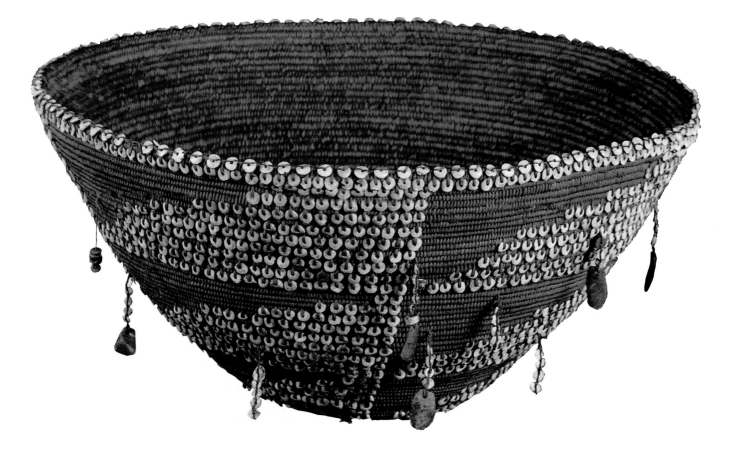

manding environment was the southwestern interior, a hilly, rock-strewn realm that outsiders regarded as inhospitable. Yet the Indians who called the desert home knew how to make the most of its scattered resources. They snared rabbits and other small game, culled piñon nuts on forested mountaintops, picked wild plums and apricots at oases, harvested sweet buds from mesquite bushes and dates from fan palms, cut cactus around the gravel beds of vanished lakes and used the flesh as a base for stews, and fortified their meals with caterpillars, crickets, and other insects.

The southern desert dwellers were among the first Californians encountered by the Spaniards. "These Indians are of good figure, well-built and agile," reported Spanish military engineer Miguel Costansó in 1769. The men, he noted, wore only a girdle, or breechcloth, made from maguey, or agave, fibers, woven in the form of a net. The women were "covered from waist to knee with close-woven and doubled nets." For hunting rabbits or killing reptiles, the desert dwellers carried a type of boomerang called a macana: "a kind of war club of very hard wood, whose shape is like that of a short, curved cutlass, which they fling edgewise and it cleaves the air with much violence. They hurl it a greater distance than a stone. Without it they never go forth to the field, and if they see a rattlesnake or other noxious animal, they throw the macana at it and commonly sever it in half."

A few tribal groups such as the Serrano and Cahuilla, whose territory extended southward from the San Bernardino Mountains, were confined to the interior. But others such as the Luiseño and Gabrielino occupied domains that reached to the ocean, where there were clams to be dug from the shore, mussels to be pried from the rocks exposed at low tide, and fish to be netted from the waves breaking on the beach.

Even greater bounty lay up the coast in the realm of the Chumash, centered in present-day Santa Barbara. There rainfall was somewhat more plentiful and the wooded hills and grassy bluffs that flanked the beaches offered dividends to foragers. From late winter through summer, the Chumash harvested fresh clover, mustard greens, chia seeds, manzanita berries, and various bulbs. In the fall, they gathered piñon nuts, wild strawberries, laurel berries, cattail seeds, and the crucial acorn crop. Along the shore, out beyond the clam beds and the mollusk-encrusted rocks, lay broad beds of kelp that swarmed with tuna, bonito, yellowtail, and sea bass. The fish in turn attracted flocks of pelicans—whose prized feathers were sometimes used to decorate ceremonial garments—along with colonies of otters, sea lions, and seals, which hunters snared with har-

A skilled hunter could send this boomerang-like throwing stick whirling low over the ground to kill a rabbit 50 yards away. A Luiseño at La Jolla owned this 24-inch-long weapon, but similar ones were used throughout southern California.

poons when they were not stalking deer in the nearby fields and forests.

To navigate coastal swells, the Chumash developed the *tomol,* a sturdy canoe up to 30 feet long made of driftwood planks stitched together with leather or fiber thongs and caulked with asphaltum, a natural petroleum tar that bubbled up offshore from submarine springs. Equipped with these seaworthy vessels, the Chumash colonized the offshore islands of San Miguel, Santa Cruz, Santa Rosa, and Anacapa. Although each island harbored a distinct band with its own dialect, villagers there maintained strong bonds of trade and kinship with the coast dwellers, and the Chumash emerged as one of California's largest and most cohesive tribes.

To the north of Chumash territory, the rugged coast with its sheer cliffs

In a California desert, a Kumeyaay man wields an ax to harvest an agave, or century, plant. Indians cooked and ate the leaves, stalk, and petals—fresh or dried. Even after five years, a soak in warm water restored dried petals to tender juiciness. The agave is a self-renewing source of sustenance; shoots from the stump form new plants.

In the 1920s, a Pomo Indian poles his boat through the tule-choked shallows of Clear Lake. Made of tule rushes tied into fat bundles and lashed together, such raftlike craft easily became waterlogged. Boatmen often had to drag them ashore to dry them out.

and dense forests offered scattered opportunities for settlement. Indians of the central coastal region, such as the Salinan, the western Pomo, and the Ohlone—or the Costanoan, as the Spaniards called them—built their villages either along rivers that led to the sea or along the few inviting bays that relieved the rugged seaboard. Those who lived near the ocean subsisted to a large degree on shellfish, gathering oysters, clams, mussels, crabs, gooseneck barnacles, and abalone by the ton and tossing the empty shells outside their villages. The relics of their ongoing feast—shell mounds as high as 30 feet and up to one-quarter of a mile across—can still be seen along the coast today.

At the site the Spaniards called San Francisco, a broad estuary linked the coast to the Central Valley, the bountiful heartland of California, where dozens of groups culled a wealth of resources from water, from land, and from the tangled marshes in between. Hamlets in the Central Valley and environs were customarily located either on riverbanks or along the borders of seasonal lakes and wetlands that were fed each spring by the overflow of the two principal rivers—the Sacramento and the San Joaquin—as well as their many tributaries.

From the marshes Indians gathered tule, a bulrush resembling cattail. The seeds and green shoots of tule were edible, but the plant was prized primarily as a building material. The Yokuts who inhabited the San Joaquin Valley, for example, and the Pomos who settled around Clear Lake near the western edge of the Sacramento Valley used tule to construct some of the largest thatched buildings found anywhere in North America. Their airy multifamily dwellings, measuring about 35 feet long and 12 feet high, were sheathed with tule mats fastened over frames of bent saplings. The Yokuts used tule mats to cover both small conical single-family homes and larger multifamily apartments. Sometimes an entire village was shaded from the summer sun by a massive mat canopy held aloft over the housetops by posts.

The long, buoyant stalks of tule, when bundled tightly together, also supplied the framework for rafts and canoes that were poled or paddled. Such rafts carried fishermen and hunters out beyond the thick reeds into open waters, where the men could set fish traps and bag waterfowl with slingshot, net, or bow and arrow. In order to lure passing flocks within range, some villagers flew stuffed wildfowl like pennants on tall poles adjacent to their marsh-side dwellings. One Yokuts band, the Choinimni, lashed tule platforms together to form barges 50 feet long, on which whole families lived during extended fishing expeditions.

Every tribe in the area had access to at least one good fishing spot. Stephen Powers, a journalist who hiked and rode through central and northern California in the 1870s, estimated that fish made up close to one-third of the native diet. He described the Indians he met as "almost amphibious," so comfortable were they in their rivers, streams, ponds, marshes, and springs.

On either side of the Central Valley rose the wooded foothills of the Coast Ranges and the Sierras. There, groups such as the Sierra Miwok and the Monache to the south and the Nomlaki and the Yana to the north harvested the fruits of

Spear at the ready, a Hupa fisherman (top) watches intently for salmon or steelhead trout in the churning waters of a fish weir. In the lower photo, a Yurok family, another northern California riverine tribe culturally similar to the Hupa, travels by means of traditional blunt-ended dugout canoe.

California's most diverse habitat. Among the hundreds of plants at their disposal were acorns, hazelnuts, bracken ferns, winter purslane, mustard, wild onions, raspberries, and grapes. Expert bowmen, often disguised as bucks in hides and antlers, stalked the plentiful antelope, elk, and deer, while fishermen netted salmon and eels, and hunters equipped with basket traps and snares woven of human hair snagged rabbits, squirrels, and quail. Foothill dwellers faced colder winters than the low-lying villagers and lived for most of the year in tipi-shaped, bark-covered lodges.

Northwestern California, with its rain forests and rushing rivers, was the domain of native peoples who had much in common with the coastal tribes of Puget Sound and British Columbia. Like them, groups such as the Hupa, Yurok, Karok, and Tolowa established rich cultures around bountiful harvests of salmon, trout, and other spawning fish. The Yurok called salmon *nepu,* or "that which is eaten," and salmon was synonymous with food throughout the area.

Most people made their villages beside misty bays and lagoons and along the banks of deep, fast-flowing rivers that cut down to the Pacific through the Coast Ranges. They plied those waters in big, graceful dugout canoes hewed from the soft, straight-grained redwood, a tree sacred to the various tribes. Yuroks along the coast made most of these boats and traded them to others. They also built imposing houses of redwood planks, split from the giant logs with elk-antler wedges. The rectangular residences with gabled roofs were as large as 35 feet by 25 feet and had plank sweat houses and other outbuildings nearby. The Hupa built similar structures of cedar. Here as in the Pacific Northwest, families proudly identified with their great houses and passed down legends about them.

Using the same kind of dip net his Yurok ancestors used and working the same waters they fished for many generations, Merk Oliver looks for salmon and steelhead where the Klamath River meets the Pacific Ocean.

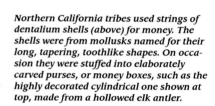

Although Indians of the California rain forest did not stage the elaborate potlatches, or gift-giving ceremonies, that were favored by their northern counterparts, they too loved to amass and exhibit precious objects laden with spirit power. Among the Yurok and their tribal neighbors, leading families collected such rarities as chiseled blades of black or red obsidian (a kind of volcanic glass), red woodpecker scalps, and albino deerskins, all of which they displayed during sacred ceremonies intended to please the generous spirits and renew the world.

In northeastern California, volcanic peaks framed a forested plateau that called for a different way of life. Although people there trapped and speared spawning fish like the villagers to the west, their take was relatively small, and they had to range far in pursuit of other resources. They skimmed across shallow lakes in pine dugouts to harvest the seeds of the aquatic yellow Indian pond lily, gathered acorns from the oaks that grew in the foothills in the western half of their realm, and snared deer in branch-covered holes along the Pit River—so called by early white trappers who frequently lost horses in the concealed traps there. Two groups who lived in the vicinity, the Achumawi and Atsugewi, were sometimes referred to as the Pit River Indians. To their north ranged the Modoc, whose varied seasonal round kept them on the move for much of the year—fishing in the early spring, collecting roots as the weather warmed, hunting in the heights during the summer, and gathering berries in the autumn before retreating to their permanent villages for the winter. They occupied their big, earth-covered winter lodges year after year, but in other seasons, they erected temporary shelters of willow poles and mats, sometimes with a thin covering of earth.

When not out after subsistence, the Modoc—whose name, like that of many tribal groups, meant simply the "people"—often formed raiding parties of 20 or so men and harried rivals. The combative confidence of the Modoc was reflected in a legend they told about Kumookumts, the creator of their world. According to the story, when he made the Modoc, Kumookumts assured them: "You will be bravest of all. Even if many people come against you, you will kill them." Although few groups in California were as defiant as the Modoc, each considered their home to be the center of the world and regarded outsiders with some suspicion. That proud

Northern California tribes used strings of dentalium shells (above) for money. The shells were from mollusks named for their long, tapering, toothlike shapes. On occasion they were stuffed into elaborately carved purses, or money boxes, such as the highly decorated cylindrical one shown at top, made from a hollowed elk antler.

sense of distinction would persist despite the efforts of priests and civil authorities to lump tribes together at missions or reservations. Like the land they occupied, the first Californians were irrepressibly diverse.

Given the plentiful resources at hand, most California Indians clung assiduously to their home ground. With the exception of village leaders and designated traders, many Indians lived and died within sight of their birthplace, never having encountered more than a few hundred people. Relations between communities were limited to a few well-defined activities. People from nearby villages sometimes came together to harvest acorns or other shared assets and to praise the powers that brought them such bounty. Some of these get-togethers provided an opportunity for young people from different places to meet one another and led to marriages that reinforced bonds between related villages. In addition, trade in salt, fish, acorns, and other essentials was common both within tribal groups and between them, allowing those whose territory was rich in one particular resource to compensate for deficiencies. Villagers in the volcanic areas of northern California, for example, had ready access to obsidian, which made fine arrow points, and they traded that prized stone for goods they lacked. Coastal groups offered their inland neighbors shell beads that circulated widely in California as currency; some beads made their way as far east as the Great Plains, where they were put to decorative use.

The bartering was sometimes interrupted by hostilities. In 1830, for example, a party of Clear Lake Pomos visited another band of Pomos to their north to bargain for

In the early 1900s, a Tolowa man prepares to measure a string of dentalium shells against marks tattooed on his arm for the purpose. Dentaliums were valued by the length of individual shells, and sometimes by the length of a whole string, as is the case here.

The beaded skirt, the buckskin dance apron encrusted with shells and hung with abalone-tipped fringe, the heavy necklaces, and the tinkling ornaments all proclaim that the owner of this Tolowa regalia is a person of wealth and high birth.

salt. A dispute arose, and the hosts attacked and killed all but two of the Clear Lake party inside a sweat house. The incident ignited a feud that halted the salt trade between the two bands for more than a decade.

Such conflicts flared up around the region from time to time, yet most Californians regarded warfare as a subsidiary activity rather than their supreme occupation. There were few prominent military leaders or conspicuous warrior societies, and threats or concessions were sometimes enough to avert bloodshed. Among the Nomlaki, the warriors were positively reticent. "They never talk about war except among themselves," one tribesman observed, "and then only in a whisper."

Safety and security came largely from self-discipline, instilled in children by their elders. An infant was born into a highly regulated world and taught from the cradle to conform to it. Men instructed their sons to hunt, fish, and build houses just as their fathers had taught them; girls learned to cook, make baskets, and tend house exactly as their mothers, grandmothers, and great-grandmothers had done through the generations. It was foolish to violate custom—a precept reinforced with many a moral tale. Children of the Yuki who lived along the Mendocino coast learned from the slapstick adventures of a character called Tarantula that deviating from the norm brought scorn. Tarantula went through life making idiotic mistakes. He tried to weave baskets out of shoots still rooted in the ground; he crawled through the earth like a gopher instead of walking along a path; he clambered onto the roof of his house and lay down in the rain to cover a hole instead of fixing the leak properly with bark. Each time he committed one of these transgressions, his exasperated wife snapped, "You ought to go off and die; you don't know anything."

Youngsters were also warned of the more serious consequences of surrendering blindly to their instincts. For the most part, adolescent boys and girls mingled frequently and faced little restraint during courtship, unless their elders considered the prospective match inappropriate. Among the Atsugewi, for example, a worthy young man intent on marrying a young woman was free to visit with her and try to make love to her. If she repulsed him with her elbow, he took it as a rejection; if she rebuffed him with an open palm, it meant that he could keep trying. Once a young couple settled down together to raise a family, however, they were expected to control their urges. They were asked to forgo sex before crucial endeavors such as hunting or medicine making; violating the taboo could doom the un-

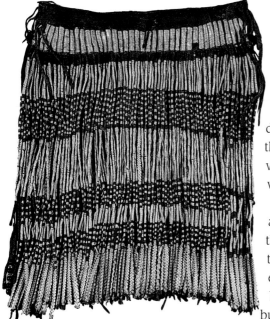

A pair of carefully woven ceremonial aprons—one for an adult woman, another for a child—belonged to a family from northern California's Klamath River region.

dertaking. There were so many of these restrictions among the Hupa that men and women slept under separate roofs and most children were conceived during a short period in late summer and early fall, when families camped out together.

Couples throughout California were urged to be faithful and avoid reckless escapades. The Maidu drove this lesson home with the tale of a foolish woman from the distant Tolowa tribe. One day, the legend recounted, this young married woman went out to gather food, carrying her baby with her. She placed the infant's cradleboard on the ground and set about her work. A large and beautiful butterfly flew past, and the woman darted after it, calling back to her baby, "You stay here while I go and catch the butterfly." Stripping off her deerskin robe and apron, she chased naked after the butterfly. She was so entranced that she forgot her child.

When night fell, the woman finally tired and lay down to sleep beneath a tree. When she awoke in the morning, a man was lying beside her—the butterfly in human form. "You have followed me thus far, perhaps you would like to follow me always," said the butterfly man. The infatuated woman happily agreed, walking for a long distance with the man until they came to a large valley filled with butterflies. "Keep tight hold of me. Don't let go," warned the man as they entered the valley. But as they passed through, the butterflies swarmed around the woman. Dazzled, she let go of her lover and ran wildly after them, back and forth, reaching for all the butterflies, never catching one. The lover disappeared, and the woman was lost in the valley. According to the Maidu who related this story, "This woman lost her lover, and tried to get others but lost them, and went crazy and died."

In abandoning her home and her child in order to pursue her passion, the Tolowa woman was striking at the very heart of her tight-knit society—the family. The Indians of California could barely conceive of a lone human being as a distinct entity. As the Cahuilla, who had 65 terms to identify various familial relationships, put it, "I am related everywhere." Or in the more pungent words of one Pomo man: "A man is nothing. Without family he is of less importance than that bug crossing the trail, of less importance than spit or dung."

Much as individuals were warned against straying from their families, they were taught from an early age to recognize and honor the limits of their home territory. Journalist Stephen Powers reported in 1877 that the tribal boundaries of the Mattole people of the northwest coast were "marked with the greatest precision, being defined by certain creeks, canyons, boulders, conspicuous trees, springs, etc., each of which objects has its own individual name." Since it was "perilous for an Indian to be found outside of his tribal boundaries," Powers added, mothers taught their children the names of the boundary markers in a kind of singsong: "Over and over, time and again, they rehearse all these boulders, etc., describing each, minutely and by name." To children growing up in such intimacy with their surroundings, everything within the boundaries was akin to them. The Maidu of the northern Sierra foothills used their tribal name to signify both "people" and "being." Humans, plants, and animals—even certain rocks with sacred associations—all were Maidu.

The recognition that the natural world was alive with kindred spirits inspired the efforts of artisans, hunters, and tribal leaders. Basket makers, for example, whose woven containers served in place of pottery across much of California and took dozens of useful shapes, from winnowers to watertight cooking vessels, saw the lovely objects they fashioned as extensions of the living plants they harvested. A woman's mastery of coiling, twining, weaving, and embellishing was only a part of her craft—secondary to her intimate knowledge of the plants that made up the basket. As an accomplished Pomo weaver explained, "The basket is in the roots; that's where it begins."

Just as basket makers needed the plants, so did the plants need the basket makers—to weed them and clip off insect-infested branches, to talk, sing, and pray to them. A basket maker who failed to do so was like a neglectful parent; little good would come of her efforts. When a woman cared for a deer-grass or sedge plant and encouraged it to grow the straight supple shoots she required, she helped the plant fulfill its destiny.

A similar bond linked hunters and fishermen to their quarry. Like Indians throughout North America, native Californians prepared for hunting or fishing by means of cleansing rituals, such as bathing, standing in fragrant smoke, and avoiding sexual contact, so that they could approach their prey free both of human odor and of spiritual contamination. A good catch depended not simply on a man's skill at stalking and shooting but also on the establishment of sympathy between him and his target. A Wintu hunter who came home empty-handed did not say, "I cannot kill a deer," but rather, "Deer do not want to die for me."

Preserving harmony between the people and the world around them was central to the duties of shamans and chiefs, sometimes called captains. In most villages, chiefs did not have broad powers, but they wielded

Photographed by a New York tourist in 1898, Cahuilla women and children take refuge from southern California's blistering desert sun in the shade of a ramada.

great influence as moral exemplars and ceremonial leaders by perpetuating observances that sustained the community. "The young chief is going to do the same as his father used to do," announced a Miwok elder at the inauguration of a new hereditary chief, who presided over a special ceremonial lodge. "Have the ceremonial house ready just the same as for his father. The young chief is going to do just the same as his father."

On a practical level, chiefs mediated disputes and offered advice, often dispensed in the form of rousing early-morning speeches. "Do right; don't get into trouble; help your neighbor," one Wintu chief advised his people

Pieced together from dozens of skins, a blanket of rabbit and wildcat fur (left) provided warmth in winter months as bedding, or as a cloak like the one worn by a Nisenan chief called Captain Tom (below).

brusquely in a sunrise exhortation. "Get up! Get up! All the people get up!" boomed the leader of a Sierra Miwok village. "Wash your face. After you wash yourself, eat breakfast. Go hunt for something. You will get hungry. After you get something, you will eat it. Get up!"

On a higher level, chiefs were spiritual guardians of the people and their resources. In that role, they were frequently aided by shamans, who claimed special powers from dreams, visions, or encounters with animals. Many groups had bear doctors, for example, who draped themselves in the pelt of that animal and used their potent medicine to cure friends or poison enemies. Other medicine men and women communed with spirits under the influence of narcotic plants such as datura—also known as jimson weed or *toloache*—and prescribed those drugs for healing. Among the Cahuilla and other desert dwellers, shamans performed ceremonies to summon rain or conjure up food, while a less exalted class of doctors dispensed medicinal herbs.

In some places, the most powerful and respected shamans formed a council to advise the chief, who in turn told the people when and where to gather plants or hunt game. Among the Kumeyaay of the southern interior, specialized shamans known as Kuseyaays were each responsible for a different local resource. Drawing on their accumulated wisdom, these shamans decided what work needed to be done and informed the chief, who then brought his people together to perform the required task, whether it was burning old growth, spreading seeds, or repairing the boulder dams that collected runoff to nourish plants.

In northwestern California, the leaders of the wealthiest families frequently exercised both political and spiritual power. The Yurok referred to such aristocrats as "real" people; many of them underwent ritual training as adolescents that put them in touch with higher powers and prepared them for the responsibilities that would be theirs when they reached maturity. A girl might assist a medicine woman during a curing ceremony, for example, and grow up to become a healer in her own right. A boy might embark on a vision quest about the age of 16 and return to his community to assist in a ceremony; later in life, he might use his family's wealth to sponsor a sacred dance to renew the world, outfitting the participants with albino deerskins and other precious items.

Reflecting her husband's elevated rank and high material worth, Captain Tom's wife wears a headband and belt studded with abalone shells and an 11-yard-long string of shell bead money—estimated in 1874 to be worth the then-impressive sum of $230.

Although leading families in the area collected treasures and enjoyed other privileges, such as occupying homes at higher elevations where they were less subject to floods, they had obligations to people of lower status. The rituals wealthy men and women presided over, for example, benefited the entire community, not just the rich. And the use of local assets such as salmon fisheries was regulated by the leaders to ensure that everyone received a share of the catch.

Lucy Thompson, a Yurok aristocrat writing in 1916, described how the salmon were harvested at a village located along the lower Klamath River. A leader named Lock installed a fish dam and nine traps on the river, aided by his ritual assistants, Lock-nee and Nor-mer. The first trap belonged to Lock and his relatives, while the rest belonged, in order of importance, to Lock-nee and his kin, to Nor-mer and her relatives, and to six other prominent families of the village. Those families would visit their traps first and take "as many salmon as they need, dipping them out with a net," Thompson related. "They must not let a single one go to waste, but must care for all they take or suffer the penalty of the law." Next the poorer people would come and take what they needed, "some of which they use fresh, and the rest they cut up, smoke them lightly, then they are dried." Afterward, either Lock or Lock-nee would open the upper gates of the traps and let the remaining salmon continue upriver, so that the villagers there would not be deprived and enough fish would reach their spawning grounds to renew the cycle.

Such management helped prevent disputes over food, but rival families of the area sometimes quarreled bitterly over other matters. Among the Yurok and their neighbors, people who had differences first tried to resolve the dispute themselves. If that failed, they sometimes called in mediators, or go-betweens, who had memorized earlier settlements and then

A Cahuilla woman fills an acorn granary with part of the autumn's harvest (far left). Once prominent in Indian villages, the large acorn caches all but vanished in the early 20th century. Yet people such as the Foothill Yokuts woman at near left, cracking kernels on a stone anvil in the late 1930s, continued to process acorns in the traditional manner.

used them as precedents for arbitration. Awards were usually made in precious shells or other valued objects, but occasionally took the form of giving up a sister or daughter for marriage to the aggrieved party, or even consigning a family member to slavery. Some people fell so deeply in debt that they could repay their creditor only through servitude. The threat of slavery served largely as a deterrent—a way of shaming the people into honoring the rights and claims of others. Parents warned children not to hurt the members of other families or steal from them with a pointed question: "Do you want to be a slave?"

No activity of the California Indians was more characteristic of their orderly and resourceful way of life than the acorn harvest. In a land overspread with a bewildering patchwork of peoples, the acorn and the rituals associated with it were the common threads. Nearly every group had access to at least one productive tract of oak trees. According to a Pomo legend, the miraculous proliferation of the oaks occurred long ago, before there was man, when the world was populated by birds who talked and acted like humans. Among them was Bluejay, who so loved acorns that he carried them about in his beak and planted them everywhere: "This way, Bluejay made sure that there would always be enough acorns for him to eat."

At least 16 species of oak flourished in California, and acorns were an important resource even in areas where the trees grew sparsely, such as higher elevations and desert lowlands. Elsewhere they were the very staff of life, composing more than half the diet and eaten every day as mush, bread, or soup. "The Indians and the acorn trees is just like the same thing," said Pomo elder Elsie Allen. "We wouldn't be the same Indians if there wasn't acorns."

In some areas, the acorn harvest was a turning point in the year. For the Ohlone, who lived below San Francisco Bay, the year began with the autumn acorn harvest; winter was measured in terms of how many months, or moons, had passed since the harvest; the summer months passed as a countdown to the next harvest.

Acorns were gathered as soon as they ripened in the fall. The bearing season for most oaks is only a few weeks, and throughout California as the leaves turned gold, the trees were monitored for signs of readiness. The Pomo looked for the tanbark acorns in their area to become loose in their cups. The Sierra Miwok of the foothills kept an eye out for early wind-falls—the worm- or insect-infested nuts that dropped to the ground before the healthy ones were fully ripe. To the south, Cahuilla hunters and medicine gatherers repeatedly visited the hillside groves located within a one or two days' walk of their villages. When they saw that the acorns were heavy, brown, and ripe, they informed the village leader, who organized a three-day-long observance to welcome and give thanks for the new crop. Of special importance were ceremonies to prevent rainfall. While rain was more than welcome in southern California at other times, it was dreaded during the acorn harvest. A hard rainfall could ruin an entire harvest, splitting unpicked acorns on the branches and leaving those on the ground black and riddled with spots of rot.

Acorn dances or "first fruit" ceremonies were essential to the harvest throughout California. In most tribes, it was a serious offense to gather or eat any of the new crop beforehand, other than for ritual purposes. Those who broke the taboo put their communities at risk and courted serious illness and even death for themselves and their families.

Once the harvest began, it went quickly. Acorn-gathering time was one of the main social events of the year. Among the Ohlone, groups of villages camped together in the groves, and the dancing, trading, gambling, feasting, and courtship went on through the nights. The hard work of gathering the nuts began at sunup and lasted all day. Young men and boys climbed into the trees to shake down or knock off the acorns. Often they used a long pole to strike the limbs, breaking off the small ends of numerous branches to effect a kind of pruning that encouraged future growth.

Beneath the oaks, women, elderly people, and children fanned out, stooping and picking up the acorns from the ground and dropping them into conical burden baskets propped against the tree trunks. When a basket was full, it was hauled into a clearing and emptied. The acorns were spread out on the ground to dry in the sun before being packed in hampers to be carried home and stored.

Staggering amounts could be collected in this fashion. Oak trees generally bear in cycles, producing a plentiful crop in alternate years; some species bear heavily just once every four to five years. Consequently, a prime harvest in one grove had to compensate for poor ones elsewhere, and the Indians toiled tirelessly when the trees were bearing at their peak. In the groves of the Central Valley, an adult could collect approximately 75

Mortar cups pit the granite bedrock at Grinding Rock State Historical Park in Sierra Miwok territory. Bedrock mortars held acorns that were pounded into meal. They were put close to one another to provide a convivial setting for acorn processors, like the Monache women shown in the inset.

pounds of acorns in an hour. A family of five could gather several tons of acorns during a two-week harvest.

It was essential to gather at least some acorns in each grove, even if the crop was meager, for plants and animals that were neglected might not give of themselves in the future. Julia Parker, a 20th-century Pomo woman, recalled that she was taught by her elders to "get out and pick and gather, even if it's only one basketful, so the acorn spirit will know you're happy for the acorn and next year the acorn will come."

In most central and southern California communities, the Indians stored acorns in capacious basket granaries propped on stilts and lined with mugwort, bay leaves, or other aromatic herbs to repel insects and retard molding. Depending on the design, storage caches held anywhere from 100 pounds of acorns to several times that amount. The huge, woven willow-twig granaries that stood beside a typical Chumash home were among the largest, containing up to 1,000 pounds. Many Shastan people of the north stored their acorns in leaf-lined subterranean caches sealed with a pine-bark covering. The Maidu of the northern Sierras and the Hupa along the Trinity River harbored theirs in large baskets placed on shelves inside their homes.

Kept dry and protected against animals and insects, acorns could be stored for a year or more. Yet the same ingredient that helps preserve the nuts—tannin—also makes them bitter and unpalatable. To render acorns edible, Californians resorted to one of two age-old methods for removing

In this sequence, Mrs. Osuna, a southern California woman living in the village of Cupa, demonstrates one method of leaching bitter-tasting tannin from acorn meal. First she prepares a shallow basin (far left) and fills it with meal. She then pours water over the meal (center) until it turns a whitish color. Finally (above) she collects the washed meal, leaving a thin bottom layer behind.

tannin. A few groups were known to bury the nuts whole for up to a year in the beds of running streams or in the mud at the edge of swamps; prolonged immersion neutralized the chemical. Most groups sped the process by first pounding the acorns into meal and then leaching out the tannin.

Among the Sierra Miwok as among other California tribes, the grinding and leaching were done by women, whose harvest came from the black oak trees that flourished in the foothills. First, they struck each acorn sharply with a small rock in order to crack open the shell and release the deeply creased kernel in its papery red skin. The shelled kernels were then rubbed together and tossed in a flat winnowing basket to remove the skin. Cleaned acorns were dropped by the handful into bedrock mortars, shallow cuplike depressions chipped or ground into the natural granite outcroppings found throughout the foothills. The meat was then rhythmically pounded with heavy stone pestles into a dense, oily meal. Women who were proficient at pounding prided themselves on never striking rock against rock, always keeping a layer of meal between the surface of mortar and pestle to create a dull thudding sound. If the rocks began to "talk," in a shallower tone, it was a signal to add more kernels.

Pounded meal was sifted into flourlike fineness, then spread in a shallow leaching basin scooped out of a pile of sand and lined with a filter of leaves, grass, or fir needles. Water was repeatedly poured over the meal for up to an hour. When it turned a whitish color, indicating that the water had dissolved the tannin and washed it into the sand, the meal was ready for cooking. Most often, acorn meal was mixed with water in a coiled cooking basket. Hot rocks were lowered in on sticks to set the mixture boiling, making a thick gruel or mush that was eaten with a shell or a spoon carved from wood or antler. Black oak acorn mush had a rich, gelatin-like consistency and a mildly nutty taste. The Sierra Miwok sometimes added crushed berries, mushrooms, cedar bark, or herbs for extra flavoring. Other groups mixed in meat, dried fish, or greens.

Acorn meal was also baked as bread in earth ovens lined with hot rocks. Some Pomos mixed the meal with iron-rich red clay, making a reddish dough one part earth to five parts acorn flour. Wrapped in damp ferns or wet oak or iris leaves, the dough was laid on a griddle of heated stone at

Two Miwok participants at a 1993 conference of California basket makers cook acorn soup by dropping fire-heated rocks into a basket filled with acorn meal and water. Constant stirring keeps the blistering rocks from burning the basket or the gruel. Northwestern Californians once ate such soup from the carved elk-horn spoons above.

the base of a pit oven, then covered with more hot stones and a layer of earth. A dark, disk-shaped, sweetish-tasting loaf, imprinted with a leafy outline, emerged six or eight hours later when the oven was opened. Alternatively, women prepared a tortilla-like quick bread, or "lunch bread," by spreading acorn mush on flat stones heated by an open fire.

The remarkable bounty that the first Californians derived from the bitter fruit of the oak tree was a tribute both to their ingenuity and to their devotion to the land and its rewarding spirits. "Never neglect my rites and my honors," proclaimed the Creator in a legend of the Maidu. "Then shall your hills be full of acorns and nuts."

Through devoting themselves to familiar ceremonies, from worldly tasks like grinding and weaving to sacred duties like dancing and praying, the California Indians sought to preserve order and continuity in a capricious world. For them as for later immigrants to the state, the land's promise was shadowed by unpredictable perils. Droughts ruined harvests, winter storms and spring thaws threatened floods, and earthquakes large and small reminded people that the powers in nature were ever volatile. Some peoples attributed the earth's tremors to the fitful movements of a subterranean giant. If he twitched a bit, little harm was done. But if he rolled over abruptly, villages might be devastated.

The many observances and restrictions of native Californians were attempts to appease such mysterious powers and ward off calamity through correct behavior. If humans did not act in harmony with nature, they were sure to reap a grim harvest. People who were careless in observing tradition, or who did not heed warnings to keep to the correct path, could fall prey to evil beings and become evil themselves. The Achumawi who lived along the Pit River spent cold winter nights around the fire in their earth lodges listening to the tales of their elders, who warned of such creatures as the malevolent Thakilmasi—a beast covered with thick hair who carried children away from their parents. No less frightening than the prospect of being abducted by this monster—known to posterity as Big Foot—was the possibility of becoming like Thakilmasi and inflicting suffering on one's people. Such a fate befell those who failed to prepare themselves in good faith before visiting holy sites like the medicine wheel—a prayer circle, delineated by piles of stones—that the Achumawi erected at the spiritual center of their world. Anyone who ventured there had first to be ritually cleansed and guided by a shaman, who urged

Slender willow shafts tipped with white feathers bristle from the tule headdress of a Pomo Big Head dancer, one of the key figures in an annual ceremony devoted to the Creator, sometimes known as Kuksu, and other spirits. The dancer wears a belt made of woodpecker scalps and holds rattles of elderberry wood.

the seeker to "keep a strong heart and hold fast to the path of life," or risk being possessed by a malicious spirit.

A similar desire to ward off evil and seek blessings from higher powers characterized the religious observances of other tribes around the region. The sacred dances with which the Yurok and their northwestern neighbors renewed the world were aimed both at preventing disasters, such as floods, and at securing plentiful gifts from the spirits in the form of salmon, game, and other nourishment. Those dances took many days and often climaxed about the time of the new moon.

Many tribes in central California took part in ceremonies of a similar character, devoted to a creator some called Kuksu. According to a legend of the Pomo, Kuksu and his brother Marumda fashioned the earth and filled it with bounty for humans. "There will be food from the water," they declared. "There will be food from under the ground. There will be food from the air. There will be all kinds of food whereby the people will be healthy. These people will have good intentions. Their villages will be good. They will plan many things. They will be full of knowledge."

The Kuksu rites were presided over by members of secret societies who staged dramatic ceremonies of curing, singing, and dancing. Observances were often led by a holy man who played the part of Kuksu himself, wearing regalia such as a feathered cape or a basket headdress bristling with feather-tipped wands that symbolized acorns, manzanita berries, or other gifts from the Creator. Such stirring performances allowed villagers to commune with Kuksu and re-create their world.

In these sacred gatherings and in the ceremonies of everyday life, the first Californians claimed a relationship with their surroundings that eluded the Europeans who impinged on the region. Intent on appropriating its wealth, the newcomers remained strangers to the land. The Indians belonged to the world, and the world belonged to them. They could face death content in the belief that life would continue for their descendants as it had for their ancestors—and that the season of their decline would bring them back to the beginning of things. An old man of the Wintu people expressed this belief in a prayer that he offered near the end of his life:

"I am falling back into my cradle.
This is what my ancestors told me yesterday, they who have gone,
long ago.
May my children fare likewise!"

A Yurok headdress (above), worn during the Jump Dance, required the scalps of about 70 woodpeckers, mounted with woodpecker and blue jay tail feathers on albino deerskin. Entire white deer hides (below)—supported on a long staff, stuffed with grass, and embellished with woodpecker scalps— were displayed during the White Deerskin Dance.

RENEWING THE WORLD

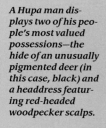

A Hupa man displays two of his people's most valued possessions—the hide of an unusually pigmented deer (in this case, black) and a headdress featuring red-headed woodpecker scalps.

The Hupa Indians of northwestern California call their ancestral homeland *natinix,* "where the trails and journeys lead back here." Traditionally they could not conceive of a path that did not return to their pleasant valley home (along the Trinity River near its confluence with the Klamath), nor could they envision a time when the land did not exist. According to legend, the valley is eternal, a home alike for spirit beings and humans, ancestors and unborn descendants.

The Hupa believe their bountiful land was bequeathed to them by the Immortals, who also passed down Indian Law, a set of detailed instructions for living—everything from how men and women should behave in marriage to how Indians should relate to all the creatures of the earth. These instructions were meant to be faithfully followed; violations displease the spirits and can produce disharmony in the form of earthquakes, floods, and epidemics as well as all manner of personal suffering. But the Immortals also provided a means of redressing such inevitable lapses—a series of World Renewal ceremonies through which the Hupa restore balance in their relationship with the spirits.

This reverence for the age-old set of laws, and the manifold beliefs and ceremonies associated with it, are shared in remarkable detail not only by the northern and southern branches of the Hupa but also by two nearby tribes—the Yurok and the Karok—whose native languages are completely different. Each fall, the Indians ceremonially demonstrate their virtue and implore the spirits to maintain harmony in the mortal world. It is a time for displaying treasured regalia—strings of dentalium shells, scarlet woodpecker scalps, rare white or black deerskins, handcrafted obsidian blades, and more—that embody spiritual blessings. And it is a time for performing the holiest of Hupa dances, the White Deerskin Dance and the Jump Dance.

With their precious deer hides held high on poles, a line of Karok White Deerskin Dancers (left) proceed from their dressing place to the site of the first dance in a ceremony photographed about 1900. Not only the dances and rituals but also their specific locations were meticulously prescribed. The Hupa dancers below take a break while another group performs.

An apron (left) made from the skins and tails of ringtail cats—the pets of spirits called the Thunders—distinguished the lead singer and his helpers in the White Deerskin Dance. The headdress (below) worn by the bearers of the obsidian blades displayed in the dance was crafted from the teeth of sea lions.

A DANCE PASSED DOWN BY THE GODS

Just before they departed for heaven to make room on earth for mortal Indians, Hupa legend has it, the Immortals left precise instructions for the White Deerskin Dance—a complex, 10-day ceremony designed to purify the people and guarantee abundance during the coming hunting season.

Extensive preparations involve setting up several ceremonial sites, preparing large amounts of food, and rehearsing the ceremonies as well as assembling the regalia and ritual clothing that celebrate the relationship between the people and the spirit beings. At a succession of places along the Trinity River, the dancers line up in front of a holy man who tends a sacred fire and explains how the dance was performed by the Immortals. Then, led by a singer in the center of the line, the dancers perform the ancient steps conveyed by the creators. Each day the dances increase in length, intensity, and splendor until the ceremony climaxes on the 10th day. Now it is time to leave the field, for now the Immortals will dance.

PAYING HOMAGE TO THE DEAD

Crocheted head nets worn by the White Deerskin Dancers are fashioned from iris fibers. The patterns woven into the nets represent maps to the heavens.

Standing in redwood dugout canoes, Boat Dance participants sing and flex their knees to make their vessels rock. Performed on the fourth day of the White Deerskin Dance to honor the dead, the ritual involves repeatedly approaching and paddling away from the shore, representing the passage between the land of the living and the land of the dead.

A feather-tufted wand like the one above—crafted from sinew and woodpecker, mallard, and bluebird feathers—is inserted in head nets worn by White Deerskin Dancers so that it stands erect at the back of the head.

Large ceremonial blades of black and red obsidian (above) signify warrior power in the White Deerskin Dance. The blades are prized as sacred relics.

A FLASH
OF THE
HOLY BLADE

On the final day of the White Deerskin ceremony, bearers of the precious obsidian
blades dance before the line of upthrust
deerskins, their blades flashing to cut away
sickness and disease from mankind. The obsidian dancers are specially trained to handle the stone, which houses a potent spirit;
legend says that the uninitiated will burn
from the inside out on contact with obsidian.

Dancers bedecked with dentalium-shell necklaces and woodpecker-crest headdresses prepare for the Jump Dance.

Necklaces of dentalium shells (right) were considered gifts from the spirit beings as rewards for obeying Indian Law. The rare shells also served as the currency of the Hupa and their neighboring tribes.

RESTORING HARMONY ON EARTH

The second major part of the World Renewal ceremonies is the Jump Dance, which begins 10 days after the conclusion of the White Deerskin Dance. Dancers form a line similar to that of the deerskin ceremony, but this time two young women—virgins who have experienced their first menstruation—join the line to perform. Prompted by the lead singer, dancers wearing distinctive woodpecker-crest headdresses and carrying narrow baskets simultaneously stamp their bare left feet and lift their baskets in prayer. At the end of each song, the dancers put down their baskets, join hands, and jump together 10 times, thus restoring harmony between the living above and the earth below. On the last day, dancers at the various sites gather at the sacred fires, which are extinguished and then relighted to signify the renewal of the Hupa world.

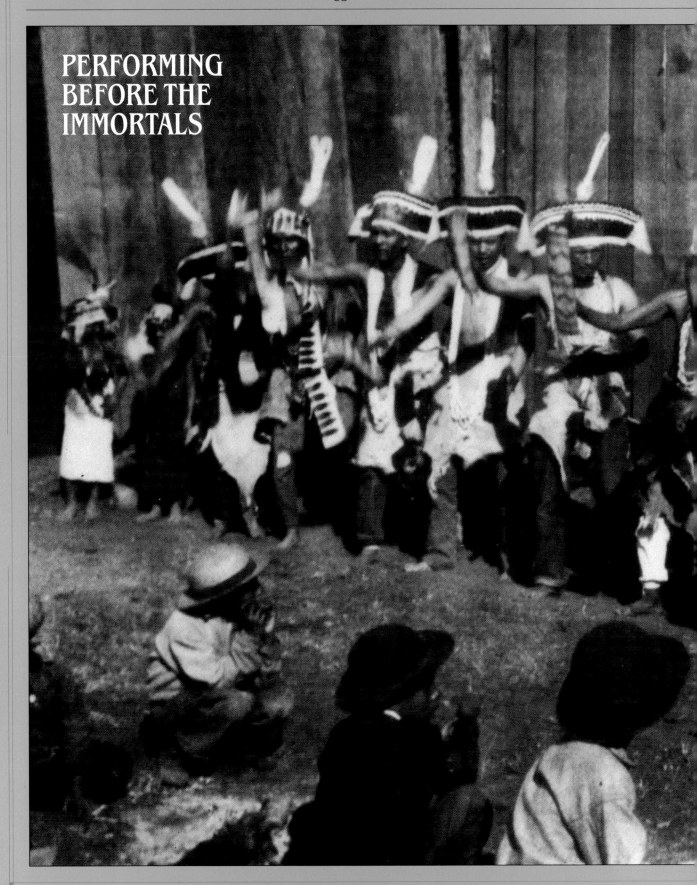

PERFORMING BEFORE THE IMMORTALS

Jump Dancers raise their baskets and stamp their feet before the high cedar-plank fence that represents a building in which the Immortals congregate to watch the ceremony. At one end of the fence stands a fir sapling in which a spiral groove has been carved to serve as a pathway for the spirits approaching the ceremonial area.

Meticulously crafted and decorated Jump Dance baskets such as the one shown below have openings along one side and, often, feathered projections on the end. Such baskets are unique to the Hupa, Yurok, and Karok cultures.

THE ESSENTIAL ART OF BASKETRY

From birth to the final ceremonies of death, the most common material items in the lives of native Californians were baskets. According to Pomo legend, when the mythical hero Marumda created the world, he gave its women *kubum*—the general term for all of the plants that could be used in basketry. Blessed with a seemingly infinite abundance of these raw materials, women throughout California made baskets for every conceivable purpose.

Wearing the basketry caps that were typical of northern California, members of a Karok family from the Klamath River area display some of their baskets in 1894.

Infants were put in basketry cradleboards soon after birth. Baskets were used to reap plants and trap animals, and for processing, cooking, and eating food. Storage baskets four to five feet tall held acorns. Firewood, roots, and other large items were transported in burden baskets; water, in tightly woven jars sealed with asphaltum or pine pitch. Prized gift baskets held personal items and family heirlooms. People wore basketry hats, rain cloaks, sandals, and belts.

Basket-making techniques were similar throughout California. Virtually all baskets were made according to one of two basic methods: a type of weaving called twining or a stitched form known as coiling. Basket makers of all regions saw their handiwork as a tangible expression of their intimate connection with both the mortal and spiritual world, an attitude that persists in the 20th century. "These baskets are alive. That's what the old people always said . . . just like the rocks are alive," noted Monache basket maker Norma Turner. "They're part of the family. They're just like one of the children."

A Yokuts weaver used black bracken fern root and rust-colored redbud stalks to create the geometric designs and rows of men and women dancers on this basket jar. Quail-feather topknots decorate the basket's outer rim.

**TURN-OF-THE-20th-CENTURY
SOUTHERN COILED BOWL**

A large coiled basket with bird and rattlesnake designs takes shape under the practiced hands of a weaver. Coiling—essentially a sewing technique in which bunches of grass stalks or thin rods are tightly wrapped and stitched together—was the principal basket-making method used in southern California.

Surrounded by the materials of her craft, a young Karok mother fashions a twined basket. Twining, used primarily to make utility baskets such as collecting containers or water bottles, consists of twisting horizontal weft strands around rows of vertical warp elements.

TWINED KLAMATH RIVER AREA BASKET OF WILLOW AND SPRUCE

COILED POMO BASKET OF SEDGE ROOT AND REDBUD

CONICAL TWINED MAIDU BASKET

TWINED PINE ROOT AND BEAR GRASS SCOOP

Photographed in the early 1900s, a Pomo woman gathers grass seeds just as her ancestors did: using a fan-shaped seed beater to knock the harvest into a large burden basket.

POMO SEED BEATER BASKET

POMO OPEN-WEAVE WILLOW TRAP TO SNARE WOODPECKERS

TIGHTLY TWINED POMO OR MAIDU BURDEN BASKET

A Pomo woman carries a large conical twined basket like those commonly used to collect seeds or acorns, suspended from a tumpline hanging from her forehead. The open-weave burden basket in the background might have been used for transporting roots or tubers, allowing dirt and debris to fall through the spaces.

TWINED POMO STORAGE BASKET

Grain showers down into a collecting basket, leaving chaff behind in a flat winnowing tray. As part of their routine food processing chores, women tossed all manner of seeds, grains, and acorns in such trays, allowing faint breezes to carry off the lightweight chaff and papery outer skins.

YOKUTS TWINED WINNOWING BASKET

YUROK FLAT BASKET FOR
SIFTING ACORN MEAL

A woman pounds acorns in an oak mortar and open-ended basket hopper. Surrounding the depression in the mortar—and sometimes sealed in place with asphaltum or pitch—a hopper prevented the acorn nuts and pounded flour from flying out as they were struck by the stone pestle.

TWINED ATSUGEWI MORTAR
HOPPER

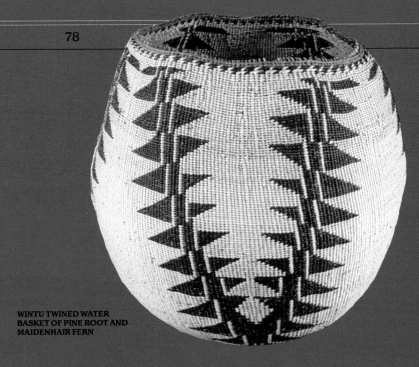

WINTU TWINED WATER
BASKET OF PINE ROOT AND
MAIDENHAIR FERN

A woman from Mesa Grande in southern California carefully pours water over acorn meal to leach out the bitter-tasting tannin from the pounded nuts. Although the one shown here is set atop a washtub, loosely twined or coiled leaching baskets traditionally were placed over shallow depressions scooped into sand.

HOLLOW-HANDLED POMO
LADLE, TIGHTLY WOVEN TO
HOLD WATER

MAIDU FEAST BOWL USED TO
SERVE CEREMONIAL
DANCERS

*Preparing food for a
Maidu feast, a
woman cooks acorn
mush in a large bas-
ket. Typically, red-
hot rocks heated in
a nearby fire were
placed in the basket
to bring the mixture
of acorn meal and
water to a boil; con-
stant stirring main-
tained an even heat.
Cooking baskets
rarely burned, but
most of them wore
out from the friction
of the rocks.*

EARLY-20TH-CENTURY
COILED CAHUILLA SERVING
TRAY

COILED YOKUTS
MORTUARY URN

A group of Southern
Valley Yokuts
women display a set
of walnut dice and
round baskets used
to play a gambling
game. The elabo-
rately patterned
gambling trays were
among a number of
special-use basketry
items of California,
including caps,
cradleboards, and
mortuary urns.

MODOC GAMING TRAY OF
TULE AND PORCUPINE QUILLS

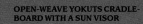

OPEN-WEAVE YOKUTS CRADLE-BOARD WITH A SUN VISOR

A twined basketry sitting cradle typical of northern and northwestern California holds this Hupa infant. A carrying handle arches over the top of the cradle. A small, separate openwork basket could be tied to the handle and draped with a skin or a mat to shade the baby's face.

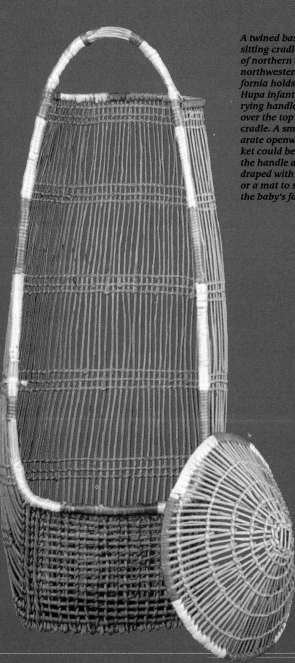

KLAMATH RIVER AREA CRADLE WITH DETACHED SUNSHADE

TWINED CHIMARIKO BASKETRY HAT

FEATHER-COVERED POMO
PRESENTATION BASKET WITH
SHELL ORNAMENTS

*The wife of a Coast
Miwok chief holds a
finely woven presen-
tation basket. Com-
monly exchanged as
gifts on ceremonial
occasions, presenta-
tion baskets such
as the ones shown
here featured com-
plex designs and del-
icate decorative ele-
ments such as shells
and feathers to dis-
tinguish them from
the utilitarian bas-
kets of daily life.*

FEATHERED POMO HANGING
GIFT BASKET

**KAROK TWINED BASKET
BOTTLE COVER**

**COILED CUPEÑO JAR WITH
FLOWER DECORATIONS**

CHUMASH LIDDED BASKET JAR

2

The twin-towered church and other surviving structures of Mission Santa Barbara stretch across a rise overlooking the Pacific in an 1880 photograph. One convert, a Chumash woman, made the straw hat above with crosses woven in its brim, possibly as a gift for one of Santa Barbara's priests.

THE IMPACT OF THE MISSIONS

"The Indians are very friendly," wrote Father Junípero Serra of the villagers he encountered along San Diego Bay in July of 1769. He had journeyed there from the Baja peninsula with a party of Spanish priests and soldiers on a mission to colonize the land they called Alta California. Everywhere the missionaries and their military escorts went, Father Serra added, the native peoples appeared confident and at ease, "as though they had known us all of their lives."

Indeed, the Indians may have known more about the visitors than the Spaniards realized. The villagers around San Diego Bay had probably learned something of the white men and their wares through trade with others in their tribal group, known as the Kumeyaay, some of whom lived near existing Spanish missions and towns in the Baja. And tribal lore may well have preserved some record of earlier Spanish expeditions that visited the splendid harbor at San Diego as early as the 16th century. The Indians around the bay knew that there were good things to be had from Father Serra and his kind: glass beads that rivaled the shell beads coastal peoples crafted themselves and used as currency, metal blades that improved on their traditional implements of stone and bone, and exotic clothing that the Indians coveted not only to wear but also to admire and exchange. Their evident friendliness reflected a willingness to tolerate the visitors for a while and trade with them. But as Father Serra would soon learn to his dismay, the Kumeyaay had little desire to live as the Spaniards did or embrace their God.

As *presidente,* or "superior," of the Franciscan friars sent to introduce the Indians to Christianity and Spanish culture, Father Serra hoped to appeal to them with offers of food and other inducements. But he found that the Kumeyaay lacked little in the way of sustenance. "The natives are exceedingly numerous," he wrote, "and live well on various seeds and on fish which they catch from rafts made of tules and formed like canoes, with which they venture far out on the sea." Far from enticing the Indians with gifts of food, the Spaniards ended up bartering for fish by offering the Kumeyaay clothing and other articles they valued.

Kumeyaays do chores amid the structures of their village in southern California. First to encounter the proselytizing Spaniards, the Kumeyaay and other Indians of the region rebelled against the invaders, attacking Mission San Diego de Alcala and killing a priest.

Such dependence on the villagers only heightened the intruders' sense of vulnerability. The Franciscans were accompanied by a small force of soldiers along with a few Indian auxiliaries from missions in New Spain, as Mexico was then known. It was a paltry contingent compared with the thousands of Kumeyaays dwelling in villages around the great bay and in the hills to the east. The soldiers quickly built a presidio, or fort, on a hill overlooking the water. The missionaries, for their part, kept close to their protectors, erecting a brushwood chapel near the stockade.

Father Serra hoped to begin the business of converting the Indians to Christianity at once, but his efforts were hampered by rising tensions around the fort. Incidents of theft by the Kumeyaay and molestation of their women by the soldiers brought an end to friendly exchanges and sparked hostilities. For weeks, only one Indian set foot inside the chapel—a 15-year-old boy who accepted food from the friars now and then and learned enough Spanish to serve them as an interpreter. With his help, Father Serra tried to break down resistance among the Kumeyaay and lure them to the chapel with a tempting offer: If parents brought an infant forward for baptism, the child would receive Spanish clothing for the occasion. The intent was that the parents would then seek conversion themselves and raise the child as a true Christian. But in taking this step, he was overlooking a principle of the Catholic Church, which held that children should not be baptized unless their parents understood the significance of the ceremony and promised to rear the child in the faith—an assurance no Kumeyaay was then informed enough to offer.

After learning of Father Serra's offer from the young interpreter, a crowd of Kumeyaays appeared one day at the chapel. Among them was an Indian who offered his infant son for baptism. According to Father

Francisco Palóu, who assisted Father Serra in his mission work and wrote his biography, the superior "immediately gave the Indian some suitable clothes with which to dress the child." Then he asked the corporal of the guards to act as sponsor and invited other soldiers "to help solemnize the first baptism which was to be administered in the chapel, with the Indians present." Just as Father Serra was about to pour on the baptismal water, however, one of the Indians grabbed the infant and ran off with him: "The others followed, laughing and jeering, while the Father stood amazed holding the baptismal shell in his hand." Appalled by such irreverence, the soldiers offered to go after the Indians and punish them, but Father Serra discouraged them. "For many days he went about with a countenance which plainly showed the pain and grief he felt," his biographer noted. "He attributed the failure to his sins; and whenever, even after the lapse of years, he told the story, his eyes would fill with tears."

This abortive ceremony presaged problems that would haunt relations between the Franciscans and the native Californians for many years to come. Father Serra and the priests who served under him were sincerely intent on saving souls. But they had another obligation that was just as urgent. Their royal commission called for them not only to spread Catholicism but also to "extend Spanish domain," which meant transforming the Indians into useful subjects of the Crown. That worldly duty, combined with missionary zeal, led the priests to adopt tactics that frequently perplexed and provoked the Indians.

The mixed motives of the priests were evident in their preferred policy of gathering Indians at missions rather than preaching to them in their villages. The Franciscans embraced this approach—known as *reducción*, or "concentration"—as a way of isolating converts from pagan influences. But concentrating Indians at missions also brought the Spaniards practical dividends by making it easier for them to control the Indians and exploit their labor. Once the mission system became well established, Indian converts produced a surplus of crops and other goods that helped support civilians at budding coastal towns such as Los Angeles, as well as soldiers at the four Spanish presidios established at San Diego, Santa Barbara, Monterey, and San Francisco. The colony's reliance on indigenous labor increased pressure on the priests to maintain a large and disciplined work force and keep Indians at the missions at all costs.

Native peoples caught in this tangled web of piety and imperialism responded in various ways. Some mission Indians took the preachings of the Franciscans to heart, accepted Christianity in whole or in part, and conformed to strange new standards of behavior that the white men equated with godliness. Others doubted that the friars had much to teach them about the spirit world and tried to make the best of a bad bargain. Like the Kumeyaays who fled the chapel with their prize, they found ways of confounding their would-be fathers. From time to time, Indians in and around the missions banded together and tried to repulse the intruders.

The first major uprising occurred at San Diego just six years after Father Serra arrived there. By then the Franciscans had won almost 500 converts—or neophytes, as they were called to distinguish them from the unconverted Indians, or gentiles. The mission, situated about six miles from the presidio, was still a rude affair. It consisted of log-and-thatch buildings, with some livestock and a few fields for corn, wheat, and other crops—a first, tentative step toward the productive agricultural existence the friars envisioned for their charges. Because of the scarcity of water and fertile land, Mission San Diego de Alcala could not yet produce enough food for its neophytes. As a result, the converts did not live with their mentors, as the Franciscans had intended. Instead they resided in their own villages, returning to the mission to attend religious services and perform chores as required. Once they had volunteered for baptism, they were subject to the authority of the priests and risked being pursued by soldiers if they failed to appear for their duties. Here as at other missions in California, a half-dozen or so soldiers lived at the site, while as many as 70 were garrisoned at each presidio.

An 1816 portrait by French artist Louis Choris features a Coast Miwok man wearing a mane of long, thick hair. Choris accompanied a Russian expedition that visited the northern California coast—one of several Russian forays that induced the rival Spaniards to plant missions north of San Francisco among the Coast Miwok.

Many Kumeyaays in the area continued to fear the priests and their military escorts, and as a result, the so-called gentiles still greatly outnumbered the neophytes. Nonetheless, the missionaries were heartened by their progress. In early October of 1775, the two resident friars at San Diego, Father Luís Jayme and Father Vicente Fuster, celebrated the feast day of their order's patron, Saint Francis, by baptizing no fewer than 60 Indians. Meanwhile, the peripatetic Father Serra and his assistants were

Using double-bladed paddles with pointed ends, two Coast Miwok Indians speed a passenger across San Francisco Bay in a fast, light canoe made of woven tule reeds in a tinted lithograph by Louis Choris. Another Choris lithograph (inset) depicts hunters of the Northern Valley Yokuts stalking game.

making similar strides farther north. In 1770 a second mission had been established a few hundred miles up the coast at Monterey, the site chosen as the capital of the new Spanish territory. Three more missions had since been founded between the first two, and another was in planning. The conversion of the native Californians seemed to be proceeding apace.

Soon after the feast of Saint Francis, however, a pair of influential neophytes named Zegotay and Francisco renounced their ties to Mission San Diego. When they failed to appear there for several days, the sergeant of the presidio and a group of soldiers went out to bring in the two "deserters," as the priests called them. Nothing could have been more provocative to the Kumeyaay. Father Jayme had warned his superiors of the ill will already stirred up by the presence of troops. At one nearby village, he said, the Indians "many times have been on the point of coming here to kill us all, and the reason for this is that some soldiers went there and raped their women, and other soldiers who were carrying the mail to Monterey turned their animals into their fields and they ate up their crops. Three other Indian villages have reported the same thing to me, several times."

The soldiers sent to round up Zegotay and Francisco returned empty-handed. Their one accomplishment may have been to arouse sympathy among the Kumeyaay for the two fugitives, who were traveling from village to village in the hills east of the mission, calling for the destruction of the intruders. It would not be an easy task. The Spanish soldiers were protected by quilted leather jackets and equipped with muskets that gave a few men the capacity to repulse overwhelming numbers of Indians armed with traditional weapons. Furthermore, California's fragmented peoples rarely conducted large-scale, concerted military actions. Still, the two resistance leaders persuaded warriors from nine villages to join forces. Plans called for the assembled fighting men—reportedly 800 in all, armed with bows, arrows, and clubs—to divide into two bodies and assault the mission and the presidio simultaneously in the dead of night. If all went well, the Spanish presence in San Diego would be eliminated by dawn.

The attack went awry from the start. Indians assaulting the mission struck first, shortly after midnight on November 4, and set buildings there afire before the second group had reached the presidio. Those warriors assumed that the soldiers in the fort would see the flames in the distance and prepare for an attack. Unwilling to take on an alerted enemy, the warriors raced back to the mission to join belatedly in the fighting there. In fact they had not lost the advantage of surprise, merely squandered it. The presidio garrison—sentinels and all—slept peacefully through the night.

At the mission, the survivors of the initial assault fought for their lives. Among those who had perished in the first rush was Father Jayme, who had appealed to the attackers in vain with the words "Love God, my children," before being struck down. Father Fuster succeeded in reaching the burning mission barracks where several soldiers were stationed. Although greatly outnumbered, the defenders found refuge from the flames in a small adobe cookhouse and repulsed wave after wave of attackers with blasts of musketry. About dawn, the discouraged warriors withdrew.

In the aftermath, the depth of Indian fury was woefully apparent. Father Jayme's battered body was scarcely recognizable, and the mission had been reduced to ashes. Other Franciscans in the area retreated to the presidio, where they remained for months, fearing further violence. Father

Indian converts, or neophytes, labor on the grounds of Mission San Carlos Borromeo at Carmel in a 1790s sketch by a British visitor. As at all the other missions, Carmel's Indian converts performed construction and other manual labor, creating a community with its own church (left), granaries, workshops, and barracks, as well as the stockade for cattle on the hill in the background, adjacent to a settlement of Indian brush dwellings.

Palóu attributed the fierce attack to Satan: "Undoubtedly, the jealous arch-enemy realized that in this territory paganism was doomed; that the missionaries by their whole-souled energy and apostolic zeal were weakening his stronghold and were little by little banishing heathenism." The uprising, he added, was nothing less than an attempt by Satan "to revenge himself upon those who had snatched so many souls from his infernal clutches." But a warrior involved in the assault gave a simpler explanation to a Spanish soldier who apprehended him. The Indians had set out to destroy the intruders, the soldier related, "in order to live as they did before."

It would be some time before the missionaries again faced armed resistance of such intensity. Word of the warriors' failure to dislodge the small Spanish force at San Diego spread from band to band and had the effect of discouraging similar efforts elsewhere. In these early years of mission building, defiant Indians could at least hope to keep their distance from the intruders and maintain their own way of life. But that possibility, too,

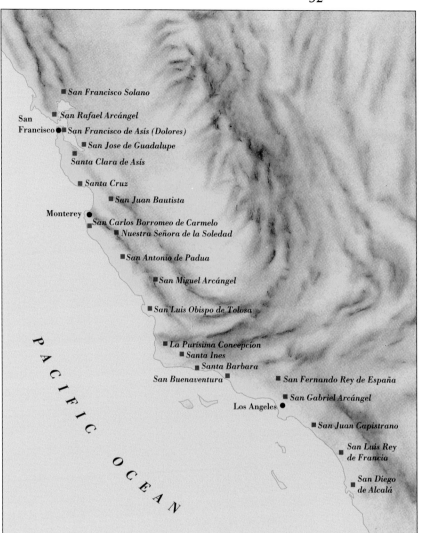

Missions founded by Franciscan friars between 1769 and 1823—21 of them in all—extend up the California coastline in a 650-mile-long chain from San Diego in the far south to San Francisco and beyond in the north, where the Spaniards hoped to counter Russian expansion down the coast from Alaska.

receded in the decades to come. By the early 1820s, a chain of 21 missions extended up the coast to around San Francisco Bay. At their peak, the missions were home to more than 20,000 Indians, or nearly all of the indigenous people remaining in central and southern California between the Pacific Ocean and the coastal mountains. Under the supervision of the Franciscans, they were asked to renounce many of their old beliefs and activities and devote themselves to a far different regimen. Rather than harvesting acorns, hunting deer, or gathering shellfish, they were expected to cultivate grains and vegetables, work in vineyards, and tend horses, cattle, sheep, pigs, and goats.

This transformation did not happen swiftly or easily. It often took several years for the two friars presiding over each mission to recruit enough converts and cultivate enough land to render a mission self-sufficient. In some cases, the missionaries scraped by through the kindness of unconverted Indians. "The principal supporters of our people are the pagan Indians," Father Serra wrote during the difficult early years of Mission San Carlos Borromeo at Monterey. "Through their sympathy we live as God wills."

From the start, however, the friars had resources the Indians coveted. Clothing and glass beads were ever popular and served time and again to draw native peoples to the missions. One Franciscan referred bluntly to such inducements as "bait." As Spanish missionaries and colonists dispensed more and more glass beads, shell beads lost value as currency in the Indian economy. Soldiers used bundles of glass beads to pay the Chumash who helped build the presidio at Santa Barbara in 1782, for example, and the Chumash deemed their own shell beads less valuable as a result. In time, few Indian artisans went to the trouble to shape and polish shells as they had before. Spaniards controlled the flow of wealth, and that wealth enhanced their spiritual authority, for Indians had long associated earthly bounty with higher powers.

As the number of converts increased at a mission, the burgeoning activities there undermined native customs in other ways. All together, mission Indians brought 10,000 acres under cultivation and raised 60,000 horses and 400,000 head of cattle. The cattle provided not only meat but also hides and rendered fat, or tallow—exports that were traded for tools, nails, glass, cloth, pots, and other items carried by ships that visited California ports. At some missions, the ranches extended for miles. Indians tending remote herds lived at outposts with chapels, called *asistencias,* where they were supervised by Spanish mission workers and visited regularly by priests. Such extensive grazing scared away deer and other game the Indians had long relied on and stripped hillsides virtually bare in the summer, leaving villagers with little to harvest in the way of wild seeds and grains. When hunger struck, the holdouts gravitated toward the increasingly productive missions, where they could count on sustenance year round. Missionaries discovered that California's Indians were especially fond of a barley-and-bean porridge called *pozole.* Lured by such fare, hungry Indians were often "caught by the mouth," as one friar put it.

The greatest force that disrupted the lives of coastal Indians and impelled them to change their ways was disease. Long before the missionaries arrived, the early Californians had been exposed to viruses and other pathogens through occasional contacts with white explorers along the coast or with Indians living near Spanish settlements in the Baja or the desert Southwest. But the epidemics increased in scope and severity as a result of close and prolonged contact between native Californians and the Franciscans and colonists. Sexual contact with Spanish soldiers and settlers, forced or voluntary, spread venereal diseases throughout the coastal population. Syphilis took an especially fearsome toll. Many women with

Following traditional ways, Indians attend a tribal ceremony in the courtyard of Mission San Francisco Solano in today's Sonoma in northern California. Native peoples who turned to the missions when their ancestral communities were stricken by hunger and disease carried on with many tribal customs in spite of the misgivings of priests.

the infection became sterile, died in childbirth, or experienced stillbirths; many of the infants who survived suffered from congenital syphilis. "They are permeated to the marrow of their bones with venereal disease," wrote a priest at Mission Santa Barbara of the Chumash residing there in the early 1800s, "for which reason three-quarters of the infants die in their first or second year."

Diseases bred in and around the missions were easily communicated to nearby villages. Mission Indians were regularly granted leave to visit their unconverted friends and kin. And the founding of a new mission occasioned frequent traffic back and forth between the mission site and surrounding settlements. A friar described the effects of one unidentified disease that struck in the vicinity of Mission Santa Clara de Asis soon after it was founded in 1777: "The Fathers were able to perform a great many baptisms by simply going through the villages. In this way they succeeded in sending a great many children (which died almost as soon as they were baptized) to Heaven." Not all epidemics were so deadly, but if too many villagers were ill at a crucial time, such as the autumn acorn harvest, the effects on the food supply could be devastating. The missions, with their herds of livestock and stores of grain, were better equipped to withstand the loss of laborers to disease, and they offered refuge to Indians whose ancestral communities were withering away. The swift absorption of the coastal Indians into the mission system was due in large part to social disintegration—the tearing apart of an age-old cultural fabric by sickness and deprivation.

Although Spanish law sanctioned the use of troops to retrieve neophytes who ran away, it expressly forbade dispatching "armed parties against the Indians with the purpose of reducing them into missions." By the early 1800s, however, the supply of potential converts along the coast was largely depleted, and some priests and soldiers bent the law in an effort to replenish mission populations by canvassing for distant recruits. Neophytes were sent out on lengthy proselytizing expeditions in the company of soldiers, whose presence had an intimidating effect. In addition, parties of soldiers and neophyte auxiliaries assigned to retrieve fugitives sometimes clashed with the villagers harboring them and conducted prisoners back to the mission to enlarge the work force. After 1800 some 14,000 converts were brought to various missions from remote areas north of San Francisco, in the Central Valley, and along the Colorado River in the south; some came voluntarily, but others were prodded into the Franciscan net by armed expeditions.

Unwilling recruits sometimes had to be induced to see the merits of a Christian life. As one English visitor observed at San Francisco's Mission Dolores in the 1820s, if any of the captured Indians "show a repugnance to conversion, it is the practice to imprison them for a few days, and then to allow them to breathe a little fresh air in a walk around the mission, to observe the happy mode of life of their converted countrymen; after which they are again shut up, and thus continue to be incarcerated until they declare their readiness to renounce the religion of their forefathers."

Such measures helped prolong a system that was meant to be temporary. By law, each mission was to render converts there self-sufficient and dissolve itself within 10 years, with most of the land going to the Indians and the rest to the public domain. The friars would then begin the process anew at a fresh site, while the former mission Indians became Spanish subjects, ministered to by ordinary parish priests. But in practice the Franciscans kept missions going decade after decade by insisting that the neophytes were unready to take their place in society; if left unsupervised, one friar wrote, they would "eagerly return to their former unrestricted habits."

Spanish officials went along, mindful that the missions with their prosperous ranches, fields, and workshops were the mainstay of the colony. Intended as a way station for neophytes on their pilgrimage toward salvation and self-reliance, the mission system perpetuated itself and kept generations of Indians in a state of limbo. Caught between a cherished past and an uncertain future, Indians adapted many of their traditions to the strange ways of mission life and evolved a culture that owed as much to their ancestral heritage as it did to the influence of the priests.

The heart of mission activity was a cluster of adobe buildings erected and maintained by Indian labor under the guidance of the friars and a handful of artisans who constituted their staff and resided on the premises. Typically the main structure was a quadrangle surrounding an open courtyard. The quadrangle had only one or two entrances, which were closed at night to keep out intruders, but the courtyard offered access to numerous

Resivimiento del Conde dela: Peí Rus en la mission del Carmelo de Monterei

Their ships anchored in Monterey Bay, French explorer Jean-François Galaup de La Pérouse and members of his expedition inspect Indian neophytes rigidly lined up in their honor at the Carmel mission in 1786. La Pérouse, voicing an opinion echoed by other foreign visitors who distrusted the Spaniards and their methods, wrote caustically that the mission's head, Father Fermín Lasuén—seen in the doorway of the church (background)—and other friars treated the Indians "as children rather than as persons of mature understanding" and subjected them to slavelike punishments.

rooms—among them the priests' quarters, the workshops, kitchens, storage areas, and a dormitory for unmarried Indian girls and young women, who were scrupulously segregated from the other neophytes at night to ensure chastity. The most prominent part of the structure was a church, usually built at one corner of the quadrangle and topped by a campanile, whose massive bells called the Indians to work or to services. Indian families lived nearby, in traditional huts in the early years and later in long rows of adobe rooms. The mission's small complement of soldiers occupied quarters on the far side of the quadrangle from the Indian residences.

For the neophytes, life at the mission was highly regimented, paced by rhythms totally unlike those they had known before the foreigners arrived. Their traditional routine had been dictated by the seasons and by necessity. They had worked hard when the salmon were running, when the acorns ripened and fell, when a dwelling had to be built and clothing or weapons made; but they had relaxed and celebrated when the tasks of survival had been attended to. By contrast, the missionaries demanded steady labor—hour after hour, day after day—often at jobs whose necessity was unclear to the Indians.

The workday began at sunrise, when a bell summoned everyone over nine years of age to Mass. Next, the converts might receive some tutelage in the Spanish language (although few ever received enough instruction to speak it well). Then, after a breakfast of atole—a gruel made from roasted grain or corn—they had to report for their various duties. Some of the men were assigned to the fields, orchards, or vineyards; others tended livestock; still others served as tanners or blacksmiths, or made adobe bricks, tiles, candles, soap, shoes, saddles, pottery, and other items. The women performed such chores as grinding meal, carding wool, and weaving cloth and baskets. Lunch, consisting of pozole, was followed by a two-hour rest period. Work then continued until 5:00, when all the converts again gathered at the church for religious services. At 6:00, they ate supper. The rest of the evening was free.

Many neophytes balked at this regimen. Tradition had taught them to conserve their energy for times when it was most needed, and even their hardest labors, such as acorn harvesting, had been marked by a festive spirit that was largely absent from the inflexible mission routine. To the friars, however, resentment and resistance among Indian workers merely underscored their moral failings. Priests viewed their charges as slackers by nature and made sure that opportunities for idleness were held to a minimum through constant supervision.

Each mission had several overseers, called major-domos, drawn from the ranks of Spanish-speaking colonists, who hailed largely from Mexico and often had Indian ancestry but proudly referred to themselves as *gente de razón,* or "people of reason," and looked down on California's Indians. In addition, the neophytes were supervised by men chosen from their own ranks, including two alcaldes, or magistrates. According to a decree by the governor of California in 1779, they were to be elected by the neophytes. Yet consensus was hard to come by at the typical mission, which brought together members of various bands speaking different dialects. By and large, the Franciscans controlled the election process and looked for officers who would do their bidding and keep the Indians in line.

A literate neophyte named Pablo Tac, who went on to become a priest, recalled the monitoring of Indian workers in the fields during his boyhood at Mission San Luis Rey de Francia: "With the laborers goes a Spanish major-domo and others, neophyte alcaldes, to see how the work is done, to hurry them if they are lazy, so that they will soon finish what

ARTISANS FOR THE CHURCHES

Once Indian neophytes had finished the long, hard task of constructing a mission's buildings, the Spanish friars assigned those among them who displayed artistic talent the task of decorating the buildings' interiors, especially the walls and sanctuaries of the churches. Many of the neophytes proved themselves expert and original craftsmen.

Schooled by teams of artisans the friars imported from Spain and Mexico—masons, carpenters, painters, ironworkers, and others—the Indian artists were soon making chairs, tables, and altars for the churches, and also carving figures of saints and painting large altarpieces. Many of the paintings and carvings have power and originality, combining Christian imagery with traditional senses of form and color. The best of them, one friar admiringly wrote, were "worthy of the praise of God."

Head and shoulders outlined by a cowl, a figure of Saint Benedict the Black wears stylized clerical robes in a simple but powerful carving rendered by an Indian artisan at the Carmel mission about 1810. The figure stood in a niche near the bell tower of the mission's church.

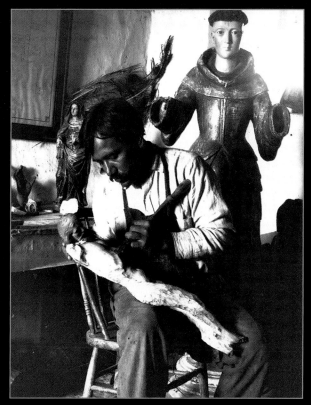

L. T. Meza, descendant of Indians who helped build Mission San Juan Capistrano, repairs a sacred image in a church carpentry shop in 1907, when a number of the missions, in disrepair for half a century or more, were being rebuilt and refurbished.

A large pink and green seashell painted by Indian artists frames the pulpit of the church at Mission San Miguel. The seashell, like many wall paintings in mission churches, was rendered using imported pattern books and stencils. From the canopy above the ornate pulpit—also made by Indian artisans—hangs a carved dove, symbol of the Holy Spirit.

The archangel Raphael, painted in bold colors by an unknown Indian artist at Mission Santa Ines, carries a fish under one arm as a Christian charm against evil. But he also bears distinctly Indian features and wears an Indian headband.

*The Virgin Mary cradles the body of the cruci-
fied Christ in one of 14 paintings of the Stations
of the Cross done from 1805 to 1810 at Mission
San Fernando on large panels of sailcloth sal-
vaged from a ship. Tradition has it that the
unique paintings were largely the work of a gift-
ed Indian neophyte named Juan Antonio.*

was ordered, and to punish the guilty or lazy one who leaves his plow and quits the field." The alcaldes did not impose discipline merely with tongue-lashings. One settler reported that they carried a "wand to denote their authority, and what was more terrible, an immense scourge of rawhide, about 10 feet in length, plaited to the thickness of an ordinary man's wrist! They did a great deal of chastisement, both by and without orders." According to another observer, alcaldes even herded neophytes to church "under the whip's lash."

Native peoples who had long been keepers of their own communities chafed at such regimentation and found ways of defying the system. Some Indians took the liberty of claiming mission produce and goods for themselves. Missionaries and overseers denounced them as thieves and complained that Indians had no sense of property. But tribal tradition made a clear distinction between the dishonorable practice of stealing from one's neighbors and kin and pilfering from outsiders. As a priest at Mission San Juan Bautista conceded, the Indians might "cheat those who are not of their own color and class, but not their own people."

Whether mission goods were watched over by Spaniards or by the Indians they entrusted with the task, all property was the priests' to dispose of, and as such it was considered fair game. Indeed, pilfering was a kind of sport, and diverting stories were told by Indians of the cat-and-mouse game between cunning neophytes and their suspicious supervisors. Pablo Tac recalled the experience of a young convert who entered the garden at Mission San Luis Rey without realizing that the stern old gardener was lurking nearby, watching for poachers. The boy climbed a tree and helped himself to a fig: "Not by bits but whole he let it go down his throat, and the fig choked him. He then began to be frightened, until he cried out like a crow and swallowed it. The gardener said to him: 'I see you, a crow without wings. Now I will wound you with my arrows.' " The boy flew from the tree as fast as any bird.

Indians reacted with a similar spirit of irreverence to sexual restrictions the Franciscans imposed on them. Especially bewildering to mission dwellers was the injunction against premarital intercourse—an act most native Californians regarded as an essential part of courtship. The Franciscans tried to enforce this rule—and keep lustful soldiers at bay—by sequestering all females over the age of eight in dormitories at night until they were married. But that barrier could be circumvented by young people intent on enjoying the same freedoms that their ancestors had. A Chumash named Fernando Librado remembered that at his mission, San Bue-

Fernando Librado, a Chumash who grew up at Mission San Buenaventura in the 1820s, holds a sheepskin blanket in a photograph taken in the early 1900s. In talks with anthropologist John Harrington, Librado bore witness to the tragic disintegration of Indian life both before and after the missions were secularized under Mexican rule.

naventura, the dormitory for the unmarried females was less secure than the friars realized: "The young women would take their silk shawls and tie them together with a stone on one end and throw them over the wall. This was done so that the Indian boys outside the high adobe wall could climb up. The boys would stay in there with those girls till the early hours of the morning. Then they would leave. They had a fine time sleeping with the girls."

Not all the traditional diversions of the mission dwellers had to be hidden from the priests. Many games with ancient roots remained popular. Pablo Tac recalled a hockeylike ball game that was played with 30 or 40 men on a side; sometimes the neophytes of one mission would challenge a team from another mission. Fernando Librado told of hoop-and-pole games, rowdy but playful stone fights between men and boys, and other age-old amusements that endured at San Buenaventura. And he fondly recalled the gentler pleasures of storytelling and singing: "I remember that the men used to sing for the women, and the women for the men, in the weaving and other workrooms."

Remarkably, the mission Indians also preserved many of their sacred traditions while embracing elements of Christianity. Their very openness to the new faith was part of their heritage, for native Californians believed that the world was brimming with spirits, and they were curious about the powers other people had access to. In Christianity, some saw much to admire. They had reason to sympathize with the sufferings of Christ and the sorrow of Mary as depicted on their chapel walls. They may also have taken hope from the promise of a better life in the next world. And they found beauty and solace in the music and pageantry they witnessed and con-

Luiseño Indians of southern California perform a dance in a drawing by a neophyte named Pablo Tac, who chronicled life at Mission San Luis Rey in words and illustrations.

tributed to on holy days. For many neophytes, however, Christianity was simply another path to spirit power, not a substitute for their ancestral practices. So strong was their attachment to tradition that many priests bowed to reality and allowed the neophytes to stage traditional dances on Sundays or feast days. And the clerics tactfully ignored performances of other ancient ceremonies.

Fernando Librado recalled that a marriage at Mission San Buenaventura was marked by three distinct ceremonies on a single day: a private Indian rite, a Christian marriage conducted by a priest, and a secular Indian ceremony, held in public. The public festivities sometimes included a rousing performance in which a male dancer called the "jealous one," wearing two pelican wings tied to his head and carrying a mock bow in his hand, burlesqued intercourse with a female dancer adorned with a cape of feathers. At one point during the dance, a singer went on enthusiastically about what was going to happen "between these newlyweds tonight."

The missionaries knew little of the significance of such Indian ceremonies—or at least, as one mission visitor put it, they would "pretend not to know." They understood even less about shamanism, for mission Indians carefully guarded the secrets of those who claimed power from the spirits to cure disease or cause it, or to perform other wonders such as controlling the weather. Out of sight of the friars, who condemned shamanism as witchcraft, Indians continued to summon supernatural aid as they always had—with songs, dances, and special costumes, such as the bearskin suit worn by Chumash shamans at Mission San Buenaventura, according to Fernando Librado.

One of the few friars to investigate and record the traditional beliefs of the mission Indians was Father Gerónimo Boscana of Mission San Juan Capistrano, in Luiseño territory. Father Boscana relied on three old Indians there who were steeped in sacred lore and allowed him to transcribe their legends and even witness some of their hitherto-secret ceremonies. From them he learned that the Luiseño worshiped an all-powerful creator called Chinigchinich, who bore some resemblance to the Christian God (perhaps as a result of the Indians' earlier exposure to Christianity). Chinigchinich created the first people on earth from clay he scooped up at the edge of a primordial lake, Father Boscana related: "Both male and female he created . . . . He then said unto them these words: 'Him who obeyeth me not, or believeth not in my teachings, I will chastise. To him, I will send bears to bite, serpents to sting, misfortunes, infirmities, and death.'" Chinigchinich commanded the people to erect a temple in his honor, and the temple became the site of sacred ceremonies as well as a refuge for anyone who took sanctuary there. As Father Boscana explained, the Luiseño believed that "as their god was friendly to the good and punished the wicked, he also would not permit anyone to be molested who sought his protection."

Missionaries sympathetic to the outlook of the Luiseño might well have appealed to them by stressing similarities between their vision of the Creator and the Christian·conception. But Father Boscana, like other Fran-

Wearing face and body paint, a score of southern California Indians, mostly Luiseños, perform a tribal dance at an 1890s festival in San Diego. Despite long exposure to European culture, many Indians have preserved their language and dances.

ciscans, believed that all pagan beliefs were a form of Satanism. Despite the willingness of the three old Luiseños to confide in him, he could never bring himself to trust in the Indians at the mission or regard their sacred stories and ceremonies as anything other than devil worship. Their apparent acts of kindness or deference he regarded as mere ploys. "The Indian, in his grave, humble, and retired manner, conceals a hypocritical and treacherous disposition," he wrote. "For benefits received, he is never grateful; and instead of looking upon that which is given, he beholds only that which is withheld. His eyes are never uplifted, but like those of the swine, are cast to the earth."

It did not seem to occur to Father Boscana that the Luiseño had good reason to avert their gaze and conceal their true feelings. The Franciscans knew or suspected that the mission dwellers remained intensely proud of their ancestral traditions, yet they asked of them repeated displays of humility and Christian devotion. Most neophytes complied, but their commitment was often less than wholehearted. And their patience was sometimes strained to the breaking point when priests tired of coaxing them down the desired path and tried to make them obey.

The friars had a number of disciplinary tools at their disposal. Any offense that was considered serious—leaving the mission, theft, fornication, insubordination—was sure to draw significant punishment, such as flogging, imprisonment, hard labor, or several days in the stocks. For a minor infraction, an Indian worker might be forced to wear weighted wooden shoes in the fields for three days, or he might be shackled to another worker. Indian women were not exempted from punishment. "The delinquencies of the women are punished by one, two, or three days in the stocks, in proportion to the seriousness," one friar wrote. "However, if they persist in keeping bad company or in escaping," he added, they would be whipped "at the hands of another woman in the quarters of the single women."

Father Fermín Lasuén, successor to Father Serra as leader of the California missions, insisted that the Indians were mostly accorded "very gentle" treatment despite what he considered their unruly nature. In his judgment, the missionaries exercised great forbearance in dealing with a "people of vicious and ferocious custom, who know no law other than force, nor any authority other than their own free will." Since the Indians were without "education or government or religion," he mistakenly con-

RITES FROM TWO RELIGIONS

Cinon Mataweer wears the ceremonial regalia of the Kumeyaay religion shortly before his death: a sash with eagle feathers and a headdress of sacred owl and hawk feathers. At top, Mataweer's coffin is prepared for a Christian burial.

In spite of the profound cultural upheaval that took place in the 1800s, the Kumeyaay people of southern California managed to perpetuate a large number of their sacred ceremonies, especially those rituals they performed to honor the dead. As did other tribal groups in California, the Kumeyaay combined some of these ceremonies with Christian elements that they learned through association with the Spanish missionaries.

The result was a compatible blend of rites from two religions, as illustrated in the photographs here and on the following pages that show members of the Kumeyaay community carrying out funeral ceremonies for Cinon Mataweer, a revered spiritual leader and the tribe's last hereditary chief.

Shortly after his death in September of 1906, the aged Mataweer was given a Christian burial by his fellow tribesmen. A year later, when according to Kumeyaay belief the chief's spirit was finally ready to leave for the afterlife, the Kumeyaay honored him once again in their traditional fashion with a series of ceremonies conducted at the tribe's Mesa Grande Reservation. At the same time, they remembered him in Christian fashion, lighting candles on All Souls' Day and at other times as prescribed by the Roman Catholic faith.

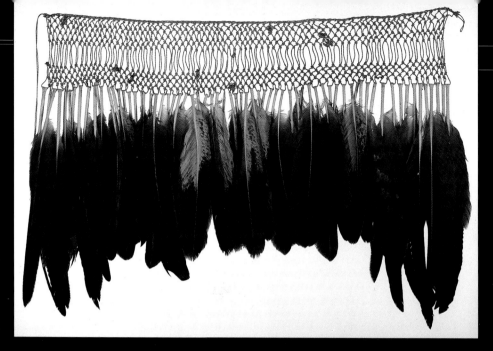

Feathers from a golden eagle, representing a spiritual guardian for deceased leaders such as Cinon Mataweer, decorate the hem of a kilt used in the Eagle Dance. The Kumeyaay mourning ceremonies were so complex that they took six days to complete.

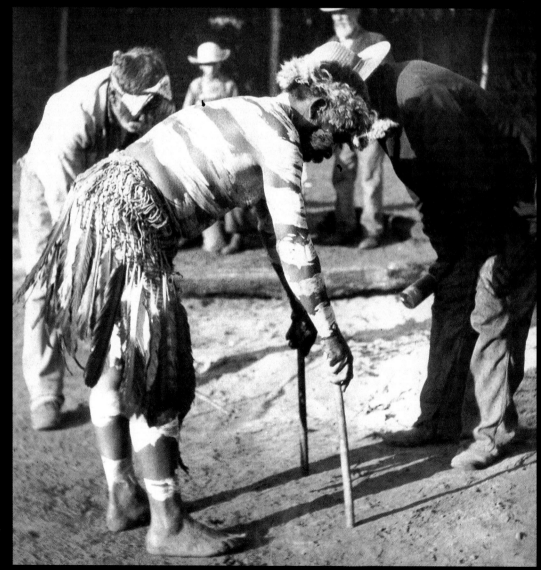

Tribal elder Manuel La Chapa imitates a walking eagle as part of the Tatahuila Dance honoring the spirit of Mataweer, a fellow member of the toloache cult. La Chapa's attire includes body paint made of white ashes striped with red and blue pigments, a headdress of crow and raven feathers, and a kilt made of eagle feathers.

At the rites for Cinon Mataweer, five Kumeyaay shamans wearing feathered head-dresses wave plumes of eagle feathers to spiritually cleanse the area. The procedure wards off any evil supernatural powers that might harm those present at the ceremony or prevent the deceased from making the journey to the land of the dead.

A ceremonial wand, decorated in this instance with an inlay of abalone, is believed by the Kumeyaay to be endowed with the power of a shaman's spiritual guardian.

Tribal elder Narciso La Chapa holds a captive golden eagle (left) that was sacrificed at the climax of the Eagle Ceremony so that its soul would help guide the deceased Mataweer to the afterlife. At right, men bury the bird with the respect accorded such a powerful guardian spirit.

Observing a Catholic feast, Kumeyaay mourners again pay homage to Chief Mataweer by lighting candles on the eve of All Souls' Day in 1907 at his grave at Mesa Grande cemetery. Many southern California Indians have continued to commemorate All Souls' Day each year, beginning their observance on the eve of November 2 by leaving candles in cemeteries to burn all night.

tended, it was up to the priests to lay down the law and discipline them: "Despite their being humans of such low grade, they are poor wretched mortals and worthy of the best treatment; consequently the gentlest and mildest means should be employed by preference."

Unfortunately, the contempt for Indians betrayed by such remarks made it difficult for like-minded priests to remain as patient and mild as Father Lasuén advised when dealing with infractions of their code. Although church doctrine decreed that native peoples had souls as worthy as those of white men and many priests acted accordingly, some friars regarded Indians as distinctly inferior and spared them little sympathy. Wrote one priest: "They are so savage, wild and dirty, disheveled, ugly, small and timid, that only because they have the human form is it possible to believe that they belong to mankind." Such bias hardened priests to the plight of mission dwellers and led occasionally to acts of punishment that were anything but gentle. Harrowing accounts of mistreatment came from foreign visitors who resented the Spaniards. A Russian otter hunter who was detained and held for a year at a California mission, for example, claimed that runaway neophytes who had been recaptured were "tied on sticks and beaten with straps. One chief was taken out to the open field and a young calf which had just died was skinned and the chief was sewed into the skin while it was yet warm. He was kept tied to a stake all day, but he died soon and they kept his corpse tied up."

It was not just outsiders who told of excessive punishment at the missions, however. Although Father Lasuén specified that the priests should never administer more than 25 lashes, the Franciscans' own reports listed many whippings in excess of that. José María Amador, a major-domo at Mission San Jose de Guadalupe, reported that an Indian "who was absent from work over two weeks through laziness or anything else not thoroughly justified suffered 50 lashes. Other serious infractions, such as quarrels at the rancherias, fights, or the use of arrows, brought 100 lashes and a set of shackles at the guardhouse." In 1799 Father Antonio de la Concepción Horra of Mission San Miguel Arcangel complained in writing of the harsh treatment accorded mission Indians: "For the slightest things, they receive heavy floggings, are shackled, and put in the stocks, and treated with so much cruelty that they are kept whole days without a drink of water." Father Horra was promptly relieved by his superiors and escorted from California under armed guard.

Coming as they did from a culture that sanctioned the bodily punishment of unruly children as well as hardened criminals, Spaniards found it

A Luiseño shaman implores the deities for rain while wielding a pair of sucking tubes, instruments imbued with power from his personal guardian spirit. For many mission Indians, the shaman remained the link to their ancient religious tradition.

hard to imagine how galling such treatment could be to the Indians. Some native peoples in California rarely if ever struck their children; others disciplined youngsters through measures that were more shameful than painful, such as switching them with a coyote tail. As for offenses by adults, most tribal groups punished conventional wrongdoers by requiring them to make restitution to their victims, while reserving the death penalty for grave offenses against the natural order like witchcraft.

In a few cases, mission Indians responded to harsh disciplinarians as their ancestors had reacted to native evildoers of the worst sort. At Mission San Diego in 1804, a friar disciplined his personal cook with successive floggings of 50, 25, 24, and 25 lashes; the Indian cook put a stop to the torment by slipping a lethal dose of poison into the priest's food. Similarly, after a friar at the Santa Cruz mission equipped himself with a wire-tipped whip and lacerated a number of neophytes, the Indians lured him outside the mission compound and strangled him.

Most priests meted out punishment with more restraint, but they could not always control the soldiers, who often took it upon themselves to whip or otherwise abuse Indians. Tensions between the indigenous peoples and the troops were aggravated by the practice of lending out mission Indians to labor in and around presidios. Attempts were made to protect women from the soldiers' advances. Yet the threat of rape, which had stirred up so much trouble around San Diego in the early days of colonization, continued to haunt the Indians. A report written in the late 1770s testified that soldiers at the San Gabriel Arcangel and San Juan Capistrano missions went out "at night to the nearby villages to assault Indian women," and that if the women were hidden, the soldiers beat the men to learn their

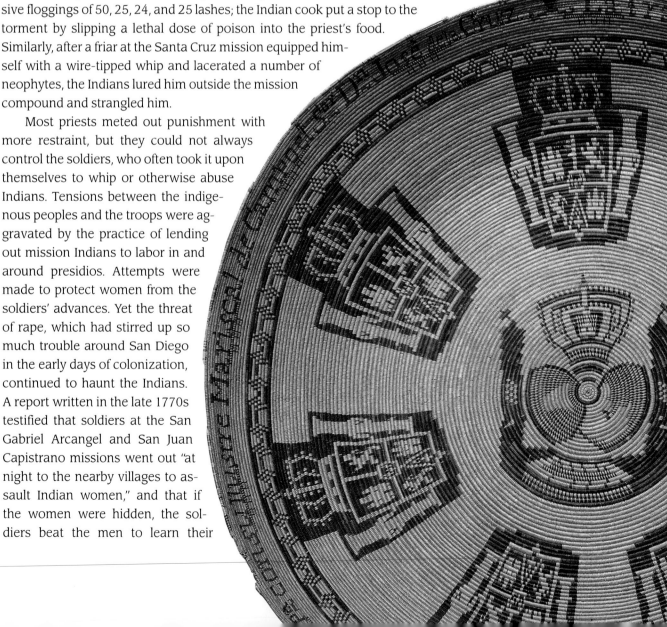

Mixing native art with Spanish motifs, this gift basket, made about 1820 by a Chumash weaver named Juana Basilia, features a crown and other symbols seen on Spanish coins. The inscription displayed along the outer edge was added in 1822, when the governor of California presented the basket to military leader Don José de la Cruz.

whereabouts. Father Serra worried that such behavior might jeopardize the entire mission effort, and he castigated civil authorities for ignoring the "shameful conduct between the soldiers and Indian women."

Some Indian women entered the missions to gain protection from sexual predation. Those who lived far from the coast were safe for a while, but after 1800, troops pursuing runaways or fresh recruits began claiming women as prizes during clashes with villagers in the Central Valley. Some of the Indian women who became pregnant after being raped or abducted reacted by aborting their fetuses or killing their newborns. According to a rancher married to a Gabrielino Indian, "every white child born among them for a long period was secretly strangled and buried."

By far the most common form of protest among disaffected mission Indians was to escape. Thousands of neophytes—perhaps one in every 10—chose to flee after spending some time in the missions. Many found their old world irrevocably changed and came back voluntarily. Others were recaptured by search parties. But some eluded pursuit and found refuge in the interior or hid out near the missions and stole livestock to support themselves. Although most runaways left their missions individually or in small groups, a few mass breakouts occurred: In 1795 more than 200 Indians fled Mission Dolores, where a notoriously cruel friar presided.

As time went on, resistance increased both among the mission Indians and among unconverted villagers threatened by armed parties scouring for fugitives and potential converts. Beginning in 1793, Ohlone bands in the San Francisco Bay area were targeted by soldiers who descended on their villages in search of runaways; some Ohlones ended up as reluctant neophytes. But replenishing mission populations in this way only amplified the discontent that confronted the priests. Uprisings occurred at more than a few missions in the decades to come—many of them led by alcaldes who chose to side with the people they represented rather than with their Franciscan patrons. The most serious rebellion occurred in 1824, three years after Mexico had successfully concluded its struggle for independence from Spain. The new regime pledged to improve the lot of the California Indians by guaranteeing them citizenship and protecting their persons and property. But the Mexican government was unstable, and amid the political turmoil, the Indians' plight only worsened.

Among the most aggrieved of the native peoples were the Chumash, whose territory included no fewer than five missions and a presidio. Grave doubts about the intruders and their rituals had been brewing among the Chumash since the turn of the 19th century—a time of terrible losses to

disease. As more and more Indians fell ill, one woman at Mission Santa Barbara had roused her fellow neophytes by telling them of a vision she had of the Chumash deity Chupu, who urged the people to save themselves from further destruction by rejecting Spanish ways. The priests learned of the movement from an informer and suppressed a potential uprising, but resentment persisted among the mission dwellers. Local soldiers, deprived of their wages during the chaos of the Mexican revolution, often took what they wanted from the Chumash and beat anyone who protested. Then in December of 1823, a comet appeared in the sky and blazed across the heavens for months to come. To the disaffected Chumash, it was an omen of deliverance.

Their revolt was triggered in February of 1824, when a corporal at Mission Santa Ines flogged a neophyte who had come from nearby Mission La Purisima Concepcion to visit an imprisoned relative—an act that enraged the Indians at both missions. At Santa Ines, fires were set and the missionaries and guards were driven into a small building, where they barricaded themselves. Soldiers arrived to rescue them the next day, but by then, many of the Santa Ines neophytes had fled to La Purisima Concepcion. There the Indians, led by a charismatic neophyte named Pacomio, had trapped the friars and soldiers in a storeroom and killed four civilians who were staying over at the mission.

Meanwhile, fighting had broken out at Santa Barbara. Under the leadership of an alcalde named Andrés Sagiomomatsse, neophytes there disarmed their guards, slashing two of them with machetes, then took guns from the mission armory and clashed with soldiers dispatched from the nearby presidio. Many of the neophytes had learned something of Spanish tactics and weaponry over the years, and they held their own, wounding four soldiers and repulsing the others at a cost of three Indian lives. After the engagement, Andrés led his followers eastward through a pass in the mountains to the San Joaquin Valley. About 450 of them settled there,

Collapsed roofs and crumbling masonry evident in the 1870 photograph above show the decay of Mission Santa Ines, which was the site of a revolt by the predominantly Chumash neophytes in 1824 and was secularized a decade or so later. At right, the restored interior of the mission church retains its wall paintings and the statue of Saint Inés over the altar.

eventually to intermarry with the local Yokuts. Another 50 neophytes who hailed from the Channel Islands reclaimed from the mission two seaworthy canoes of Chumash design called tomols and fled to Santa Cruz Island.

The 400 rebels at La Purisima Concepcion chose not to retreat. Instead, they turned the mission into a fortress, complete with freshly cut firing slits and a pair of swivel guns. The government's response came a few weeks later. More than 100 Mexican troops hammered through the Indians' defenses with cannon, killing 16 of the rebels with the loss of only one soldier. Pacomio was sentenced to 10 years of labor at the local presidio.

Other revolts of lesser magnitude occurred during the tumultuous early years of Mexican independence. In 1827, for example, an alcalde from Mission San Jose led 400 neophytes into the interior. A year later, another San Jose alcalde recruited neophytes from several missions in the area for a planned uprising and raided the outlying ranches for horses; the leader eventually gave himself up, however.

By then the mission system was nearing its end. The first Mexican governor of California proposed the abolition of the missions—most of which had been in existence for far longer than the 10 years originally called for. The Franciscans responded by restating their old arguments against trying to fold the Indians into the Hispanic population. But the growing contingent of Mexican civilians in California now began to express an interest in the matter. These gente de razón were land hungry, eager to get their hands on the immense holdings of the missions. Spanish and Mexican authorities had granted civilians title to only 50 or so ranches by the early 1830s, and their combined area was small compared with

Indian herdsmen tend sheep near the crumbling Mission La Purisima Concepcion after the mission—another site hit by the revolt of 1824—was sold as a ranch some two decades later. By then only about 200 Indians from the mission remained, and all its buildings had collapsed except for the monastery seen below, which was used as a stable.

the nearly eight million acres covered by the missions. Hide and tallow from grazing cattle remained California's leading trade, and ambitious Mexicans who no longer felt beholden to the Franciscans resented the fact that they still dominated the market.

In 1834 a new governor of California, backed by an edict from Mexico City, finally secularized the missions, freeing the Indians from the hold of the Franciscans but exposing them to harsh new pressures. At first glance, the secularization decree appeared to benefit the neophytes. The mission grounds were to be converted into pueblos, or towns, served by parish priests; the surrounding land was to be distributed to the neophytes, with each adult male or head of a family receiving 33 acres. Half of each mission's livestock, tools, and seeds were also to go to the neophytes. But the law contained a number of clauses that spelled trouble for the Indians. All surplus land, livestock, tools, and other property were to become the responsibility of administrators appointed by the governor—and these same officials could require the neophytes to work the undistributed lands as well as their own plots. Forced labor was deemed a necessity in a land where Indians still greatly outnumbered Mexicans and produced most of the wealth. As one Franciscan expressed it: "If there is anything to be done, the Indian has to do it; if he fails to do it, nothing will be done."

Of the millions of acres of land released by secularization, the Indians retained little. Here and there, groups of former mission Indians maintained communities around their old places of worship, applying irrigation techniques and other useful skills they had learned from the Franciscans and practicing a form of Christianity that harmonized with their ancestral traditions. But few of the ex-neophytes were so fortunate. Some were defrauded of their holdings; some gambled them away. In most cases, the appointed administrators simply took private possession of mission buildings, equipment, livestock, and other "surplus" assets and used the acquired wealth as a lever to separate Indians from their holdings. A former neophyte at Mission San Luis Rey recalled how the civil administrator there, Don Pío Pico, expanded his estate. At first he bought land, "paying for it with the same cattle which he had appropriated from the mission." But as his power and influence increased, he simply seized unclaimed land and the property of the surrounding Indians, who had little recourse against a wealthy Mexican with the authorities on his side. In time, the Pico family estate swelled to 700,000 acres.

The big landowners inherited a significant portion of the former work force of the missions, employing about 4,000 Indians in all. Although grain was cultivated at the ranches, the main activities were herding cattle, tanning hides, and rendering tallow—skills for which the Indian vaqueros, or cowhands, had been well trained at the missions. Their payment consisted mainly of shelter and food, and the bosses saw to it that most workers had to go into debt to meet the larger needs of their families. By law, they could not leave their employers if they were indebted to them, and many Indians were reduced to a condition of peonage, or virtual servitude.

Other displaced Indians sought employment in towns that had grown up along the coast during the mission period. Native peoples from the missions of San Diego, San Luis Rey, and San Juan Capistrano, for example, headed for Los Angeles to join unconverted Indians who had found a toehold there by laboring for vineyards and other budding enterprises. Between 1830 and 1836, the number of Indians living in Los Angeles grew from 198 to 533, or nearly one-fourth of the town's population. Many of these newcomers were unable to find work, however, and took to drinking heavily. This led to employment of a sort: Town councilmen arrested Indians for drunkenness and put them to work on public projects—a new variation on the forced labor that had long been the basis of California's economy. The local Indians had alcaldes, who did their best to protect them. In 1838 the alcaldes successfully petitioned town officials to remove a white man who had settled on land assigned to the Indians. But the years ahead saw the native Angelenos deprived of what few rights they had. In 1847 the Indian district there was razed. Residents who had jobs as servants were required to live with their masters, others who appeared to be self-sufficient were forced outside the city limits, and those deemed vagrants were relegated to jail or public works.

Many of the ex-neophytes who did not flock to the towns or fall under the sway of the land barons drifted into the interior, which remained largely the province of native Californians. It was not easy for Indians who had lived at missions to find a home amid alien tribal groups and revert to traditional subsistence patterns. Some made a living by rustling cows and horses from the ranchers and eating the meat or trading away the livestock. The land barons and Mexican authorities responded to such raids with punitive expeditions. As in the past, these armed parties often included Indian auxiliaries, and some were dispatched not only to pursue wrongdoers but to corral Indian laborers for the big estates—now fast expanding as the government issued land grants in the interior.

During this chaotic time of raids, reprisals, and enslavement, barbarous deeds occurred. In 1837 José María Amador—formerly a mission

A survivor of turbulent times, a Yokuts matriarch sits surrounded by some of her descendants in this picture taken about 1900. As a child, she was taken from her Central Valley homeland to Mission San Juan Bautista, near present-day Salinas, only to be caught in the upheaval of secularization.

major-domo and now a rancher—led a party of civilians, soldiers, and Indian auxiliaries on an expedition into the San Joaquin Valley. They came upon a camp of suspected wrongdoers, including 100 or so former neophytes and a comparable number of unconverted Indians. Amador wrote that he "invited the wild Indians and their Christian companions to come and have a feast of pinole and dried meat." The Indians gladly accepted and crossed a river where the armed members of the expedition were waiting for them on the far bank and quickly subdued them. Before leading the captives back to their camp, Amador and others separated out the Christians. "At every half-mile or mile, we put six of them on their knees," he revealed, "making them understand that they were about to die. Each one was shot with four arrows, two in front and two in the back. Those who refused to die immediately were killed with spears. On the road were killed in this manner the 100 Christians."

Back at the camp, Amador decided to execute the unconverted prisoners—after he first baptized them with the help of an aide: "I ordered Nazario Galindo to take a bottle of water and I took another. He began at one part of the crowd and I at another. We baptized all the Indians and afterwards they were shot in the back. At the first volley, 70 fell dead. I doubled the charge for the 30 who remained, and they all fell."

Such murderous expeditions were not the only threats to Indians in the Central Valley. A few years earlier, trappers for the Hudson's Bay Com-

San Antonio de Pala (top) originated in 1816 as an asistencia for nearby Mission San Luis Rey and has continued to serve as a place of worship ever since, presently as part of the Pala Indian Reservation. At bottom, Cupeño women pray in Pala's chapel not long after it received a whitewashing in 1903.

pany had ventured down from Oregon, introducing malaria into the marshy interior lowlands. The disease killed an estimated 20,000 Indians and remained endemic thereafter. The native peoples who endured had to reckon with further intrusions by trappers, who not only filtered down from the north but found their way into California on trails through or around the Sierras. These beaver hunters remained on generally good terms with the Indians of the interior, but other Americans who followed them nursed ambitions that would soon put them at odds with native Californians. They launched careers as merchants, traders, and ranchers. Many converted to Roman Catholicism, acquired Mexican citizenship, and married into local families; some even took Spanish names.

Not all the newcomers were willing to adapt in this way, however. Some disputed Mexico's right to possess this land of abundance. A New Englander named John Marsh arrived in 1836, bought a large ranch in the San Joaquin Valley, and, within a few years, began urging the U.S. government to annex California. He saw the takeover as inevitable. In the early 1840s, pioneers began streaming in by way of a branch of the Oregon Trail, prompting Marsh to write to a U.S. senator that California "cannot long remain in the hands of its present owners." He did not credit the Indians as rightful owners. Their role, he insisted, was to serve the Americans as they had the Spaniards and Mexicans. "When caught young," he wrote, the Indians are "easily domesticated, and manifest a great aptitude to learn whatever is taught them. Nothing is more necessary for their complete subjugation but kindness in the beginning, and a little well-timed severity when manifestly deserved." Marsh gave the local Indians food and clothes—but no pay—in return for cultivating his fields and helping to build his ranch house.

The most imposing enterprise built up by a foreigner was that of a German-born Swiss immigrant named Johann August Sutter, who reached California in 1839 after suffering various business failures elsewhere in the New World. A year later, he received Mexican citizenship and a large land grant of 50,000 acres near present-day Sacramento. Sutter was a man of bold talk and big ideas. He gave his estate the name of New Helvetia—New Switzerland—and ran it as his personal fiefdom. Here as elsewhere, Indians provided the labor, cultivating wheat, tending Sutter's vast herds, constructing adobe buildings that included a fort, and operating a distillery, a tannery, a hat factory, and a blanket-making shop. Their usual compensation was food, shelter, and clothing. Like Indian workers on the cattle ranches, most of them fell into debt and found themselves at

Sutter's mercy. If they refused to cooperate, they might be whipped, jailed, or even executed. To suppress any resistance on or around the estate, Sutter picked out Indians he felt could be trusted and created his own private army, consisting of 150 infantrymen and 50 cavalrymen, all dressed in green-and-blue uniforms. The army was led by white officers, who issued their basic commands in German.

Westward-bound Americans who stopped at Sutter's estate as they neared the end of their long overland journey were generally impressed by Sutter's control over his Indian work force. Explorer John Charles Frémont noted approvingly that, although Sutter initially had some difficulties with the local Indians, "by the occasional exercise of well-timed authority, he had succeeded in converting them into a peaceable and industrious people." A few visitors regarded his treatment of the native peoples with extreme distaste, however. One complained that Sutter "keeps 600 or 800 Indians in a complete state of Slavery" and told of seeing them fed from troughs that were brought from the cookhouse and placed in the broiling sun. A disgruntled employee claimed that Sutter had sexual relations with Indian girls as young as 10. That charge may not have been true, but Sutter certainly looked to Indian women for his private pleasures.

In his dealings with Indians, Sutter embodied the spirit of exploitation that continued unabated even as Americans wrested control of California from the Mexicans. The change was set in motion by the Mexican War, a long-threatened showdown between an expansionist United States and its land-rich but weaker neighbor to the south. The war was a relatively bloodless affair in California, where the Mexican government lacked the resources to present much resistance to the American troops who invaded in 1846 and claimed the territory, two years before it was formally ceded to the United States. Americans proclaimed the outcome a triumph for liberty, but not much changed for the Indians. New Helvetia made it through this transitional period without much difficulty. When a measles epidemic struck the Sacramento Valley in 1847 and decimated Sutter's work force, he simply resorted to the old expedient of rounding up "wild" Indians as replacements.

Native peoples would derive no benefit from the pending admission of California to the Union as a so-called free state. For the lot of the Indians was seldom improved by the lofty ideals of those who claimed authority over them. Whether the intruders were Catholics or Protestants, priests or profit seekers, most regarded Indians as mere instruments of their own will or God's will, to be put to convenient use, if possible. Indeed, the long

Troops of Johann August Sutter's private Indian militia, used to protect the rancher's vast properties, drill outside his fortresslike house overlooking lush fields in what is now Sacramento. The discovery of gold near Sutter's land triggered the 1849 rush to California that helped dispossess the Indians of much of what remained of their native land.

nightmare of the original Californians was about to intensify with the arrival of men who had no use for the Indians at all and simply wanted them out of the way. There were still as many as 125,000 Indians living in California—far more Indians than there were white people. Many tribal groups in the rugged north and in the Sierra foothills adhered to their old ways. But soon there would be no refuge. Soon even the remotest mountain valleys would be overrun by white fortune hunters.

Indirectly, Johann August Sutter triggered the invasion. On Monday, January 24, 1848, an odd gleam was spotted in the millrace of a sawmill that was being constructed for Sutter with the help of Indian laborers in the foothills along the South Fork of the American River, east of Sutter's estate. The overseer in charge of the project shut off the race. As the current ceased, he stepped into the water, plucked some samples from the bottom, and inspected them closely. In his hand lay a prize that would bring native Californians incalculable misfortune—gold.

EXILE FOR THE CUPEÑO

"At Cupa we lived well," explained Rosinda Nolasquez, a Cupeño Indian whose people were evicted from their ancestral land in 1903, when she was a child. Some 60 years after the move, she recalled growing up in a virtual Eden where apple, pear, peach, apricot, and almond trees bloomed beside bubbling hot springs.

Cupeño tradition holds that her ancestors settled the village of Cupa, located in present-day San Diego County, not long after the creation of the world; European accounts confirm that the Indians were well established there when the first Spanish settlers arrived in 1795. At the village was much that the people held sacred, including the graves of their forefathers and the bountiful sulfur springs. Not only did the Cupeño treasure the springs for their curative powers, they also believed them to be the home of a fierce leviathan called Mawepish and other supernatural beings who influenced the tribe's fate.

Even after the governor of California denied the Indians' sovereignty and ceded the land they lived on to a rancher named Juan José Warner in 1844, the Cupeño remained at Cupa, renamed Warner's Hot Springs, and worked for pitiful wages. One observer described their condition under Warner as "worse by far than the worst-treated slaves in the United States." Neglect and exploitation so incensed the Indians that in 1851 they staged an uprising. Although the revolt was quelled and many of the leaders were executed, Warner abandoned the ranch and eventually the land fell into the hands of another rancher, John G. Downey, whose family sued for removal of the native "interlopers" in 1893.

The Cupeño, however, refused to budge. They fought a bitter legal battle to retain their homeland, taking their claim all the way to the California Supreme Court. After a protracted struggle, the court settled against them in 1902. When asked where they would like to move, Captain Cibimoat, a chief, answered through a translator: "You see that graveyard out there? There are our fathers and grandfathers. We have always lived here. We would rather die here. Our fathers did. We cannot leave them.

Our children were born here. How can we go away? We do not want any other home."

Despite Cibimoat's impassioned plea, in 1903 the federal government moved the tribe to a 3,438-acre reservation at Pala, a former mission branch in the territory of the Luiseño Indians, located about 40 miles northwest of their old home. Although the new territory was fertile, some of the older Cupeños steadfastly refused to go. According to tribal history, at least one great-grandmother fled into the hills, shouting, "Here I will stay, even if I die, even if coyotes eat me." The remaining 98 Indians made the exhausting journey to an unfamiliar home, documented on the following pages.

Cupeño Indians meet with members of the Sequoya League in front of a thatched house at Cupa in 1902. Founded by Indian advocate Charles Lummis to aid the Indians of southern California, the league rejected several sites as unsuitable before recommending Pala as a new home for the tribe.

Cupeño women load household goods onto a wagon in preparation for their journey. Cargo space was limited, so many items had to be left behind. Rosinda Nolasquez, who was a child at the time, remembered having to put up a fight to bring her pet cats.

Captain Cibimoat hitches up his horse. A photographer on the scene described the chief's departure: "While I helped him hitch a bony mustang to his buggy, a tear or two coursed down his knife-scarred face; and as the teamsters tore down his little board cabin wherein he had kept a restaurant, he muttered, 'May they eat sand!' "

Cupeño women and children bid farewell to the graves of their forebears. Rosinda Nolasquez remembered people weeping when an official told them to go to the cemetery to "see your relatives for the last time now. You're never going to see them again."

A wagon train leaves Cupa on Tuesday, May 12, 1903, escorted by government agents. According to one Cupeño participant: "No one turned around. They kept going on westward. They did not look back again."

*Cupeños unpack their belongings, including pieces of bas-
ketry, when their wagons stop for lunch during the three-
day journey to Pala. Some of the Indians preferred to eat
their own provisions rather than the government-supplied
rations, insisting proudly that they did not accept charity.*

*The Cupeño wagon train winds its way along dusty moun-
tain roads. A group of about a dozen young Indians
followed the train on horseback, driving a small herd of
cattle and ponies that the people took with them.*

Women and children settle with reluctance into their new home, a temporary tent village erected on the banks of the San Luis Rey River at Pala. The transplants complained bitterly about having to live among "fleas and squirrels" in the alien valley.

Newly arrived Cupeño men gather on a makeshift log bridge to examine a stream that supplied water at Pala. The federal government paid the men two dollars a day plus rations to build a village and dig irrigation ditches that diverted water from mountain streams to their farm and grazing land.

A panoramic view of Pala shows rows of prefabricated frame houses, shipped to the reservation several months after the arrival of the Cupeños. These structures proved more expensive and less sturdy than the adobe buildings the Indians had left behind. In addition, one new resident lamented that the homes were "as tiny as beehives."

Dressed in traditional festive attire, Cupeños parade through the streets of Pala on June 2, 1913, to celebrate the opening of a new irrigation system and pumping station. A local official announced at the ceremony that the U.S. government had granted the people, after 10 years of residency at Pala, absolute title to their lands.

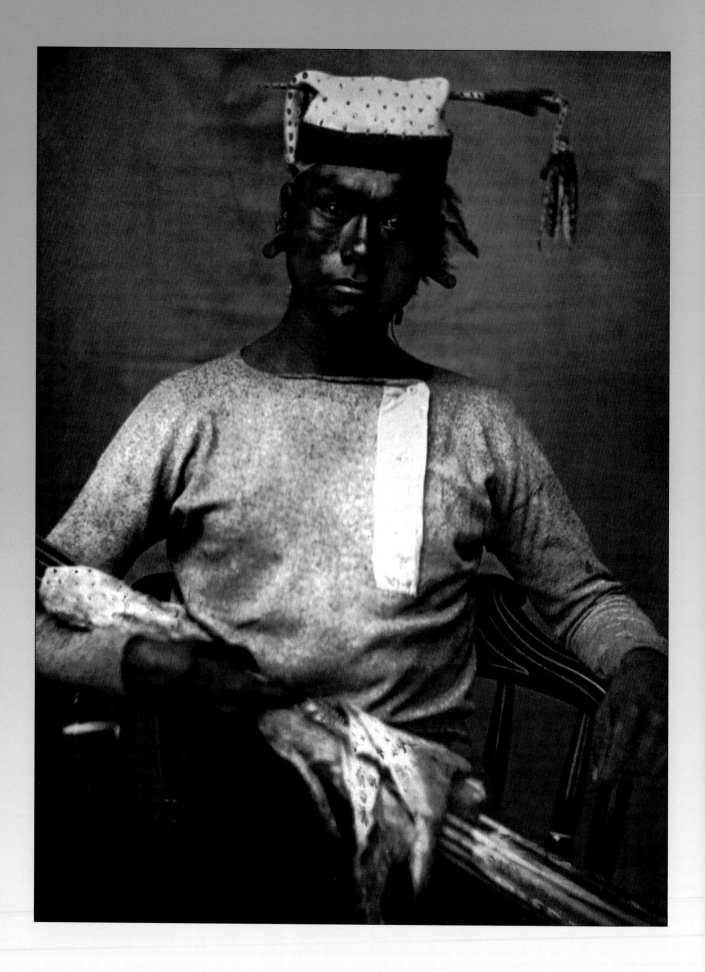

3

CULTURES IN A STRUGGLE TO SURVIVE

A Nisenan man in clothing adapted from the whites pouring into his territory holds a quiver full of arrows in this 1850 photograph, one of the earliest taken of a California Indian. The Nisenan were devastated by the impact of the gold rush, which brought an avalanche of fortune seekers down on their homeland in the Sierra foothills.

For millennia, Indians living among the foothills of the Sierra Nevada ignored the flecks of gold that glinted from gullies, creek beds, and riverbanks. Much of the ore was in placer form—loose particles that had crumbled away from veins high in the mountains and been carried downhill by wind and rain. Although these alluvial deposits could easily have been mined by the Indians, gold was too soft to be crafted into tools or weapons and so held little interest for them. The native Californians who worked for Johann August Sutter—mostly Miwoks and Nisenans—thus had no inkling of how profoundly their lives would be changed by the discovery of gold in his millrace along the South Fork of the American River in January 1848.

Lacking any claim to the mill site, Sutter appealed to some Nisenans who lived nearby and offered them food and clothing if they would grant him use of the land for three years—long enough, presumably, to extract its riches. Sutter cared little for the prerogatives of the Indians, but he hoped to use this lease, as he called it, to forestall other white fortune hunters. His plans were frustrated when Colonel Richard B. Mason, military governor of California, refused to acknowledge the deal. "The United States," he declared, "does not recognize the right of Indians to sell or lease their lands." Far from constituting a promise to defend Indians from fraud and encroachment, Colonel Mason's words foretold further indignities for the native Californians: Once again, outsiders would treat them as aliens in their own land and define their rights for them.

Sutter had hoped to keep the discovery of gold at the millrace secret, but the news leaked out and swiftly spread. By the end of May, fully half of San Francisco's 800 residents had fled town to pan for the precious ore in the rivers, streams, and creeks that cut down through the foothills at the eastern edge of the Central Valley. As word spread, thousands of miners flocked to the region—some from Oregon and others from as far away as Mexico and South America. An official at Monterey complained in disgust that "the farmers have thrown aside their plows, the lawyers their briefs, the doctors their pills, the priests their prayer books, and all are now digging gold." Soon, Americans back east were gripped by gold fever, and adventurers were crossing over from Europe to join in the pursuit. "The coming of the Messiah or the dawn of the Millennium would not have excited anything like the interest," exclaimed one newspaper editor.

Sutter himself was ruined by the gold rush. Many of his white supervisors left him to prospect for gold, and once they were gone, there was little to hold back his Indian laborers.

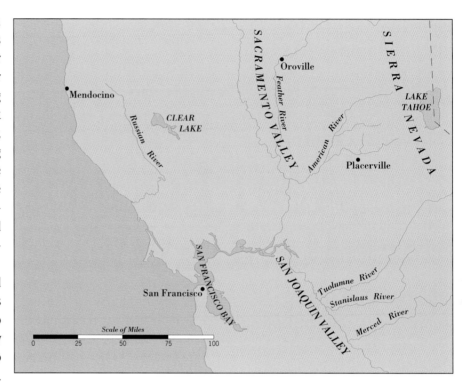

Lured by the news of gold strikes in 1848, prospectors surged into central California to sift for the precious ore along the rivers and creeks that flowed down from the mountains into the Sacramento and San Joaquin Valleys. As they moved to stake their claims, the newcomers created boom towns in the foothills and brought death and dislocation to countless Indian communities.

His revenues dwindling, Sutter was soon forced to carve up and sell off his vast estate. "What a great misfortune was this sudden discovery of gold for me," he lamented in later years. He recalled that some of his Indian workers had warned him that gold was bad medicine. And so it proved to be, not only for Sutter but for tens of thousands of native Californians whose rich legacy would be imperiled by the onslaught of prospectors.

Nothing in recent times quite prepared California's Indians for the havoc to come. For while Spaniards and Mexicans had claimed their souls and commanded their labor, the American fortune hunters coveted their land and its wealth and wanted the Indians themselves removed or eliminated. The discovery of gold sparked what one American official termed a "war of extermination," one that would continue for more than two decades. Indian men, women, and children would be assaulted in their villages and driven from their lands onto barren reservations. Time and again, resistance would flare up among native groups, only to be brutally extinguished. Many of those subdued by the intruders would labor as virtual slaves in a free state. Yet resilient communities of native Californians would endure this long trial by fire, until they reclaimed their neglected heritage and hope began to flower anew.

At first, the impact of gold on the lives of Indians was deceptively benign. Many of those who had once toiled as ranch hands or servants for whites simply labored as miners for the same men. Others hired themselves out to prospectors who were new to the territory. Entire Indian families worked the placers, scooping up ore-laden gravel from riverbanks and deftly panning it in special wooden bowls or reed baskets. For their efforts, they were usually rewarded with just enough food and clothing to keep them working. The gold went to the employer. Those few Indian miners who were paid in gold or coin were lucky to get one dollar a day, while the whites profited hugely. On the Feather River, north of the American, 50 Indians turned up 273 pounds of gold in less than two months for a group of seven whites from Monterey. After covering their expenses with an outlay of about 14 pounds of gold, each of the partners went home with 37 pounds of gold worth more than $9,000.

Some prospectors amassed fortunes with the help of small armies of Indian laborers. Charles Weber, a former supervisor for Sutter, worked out an arrangement with Yokuts leaders that brought Weber and his partners the services of hundreds of Yokuts; by one account, Weber and company had 1,000 Indians toiling for them on Weber's Creek, near Placerville. To the south, in present-day Calaveras County, a prospector named John Murphy forged ties with the Miwok by marrying the daughter of a tribal chief. He retained the labor of perhaps 600 Indians, most of them Miwoks, and pitched his tent in their midst, bringing with him a herd of cattle to feed the workers. The Indians would "gather gold for him and receive in return provisions and blankets," one visitor observed. "He knocks down two bullocks a day to furnish them with meat."

Soon, some Indian miners became aware of the value of their labor and began to demand fair compensation, often in gold or coin. One white woman complained that the Nisenans who were panning gold for her husband refused to work for trifles as they had before. They had toiled day in and day out for "next to nothing," as she put it, having been assured by their employers that "gold was stuff to whitewash houses with." Now they knew better and wanted more than a handkerchief for a tin cupful of precious ore. Some Indians struck out on their own, preferring to keep the gold they mined and exchange it for what they wanted rather than trust an employer to treat them fairly. But they risked being cheated by the gold merchants as well, some of whom tipped the scales against Indians by employing a so-called Digger ounce, a two-ounce counterweight that resembled the standard one-ounce measure.

Miners, many of them Indians, dig for gold at Taylorsville in 1849, when whites were beginning to drive Indians away from the rich sites. One mine owner told of being harassed by prospectors from Oregon, who "protested against my Indian labor. I then left the stream and returned to my home."

By December 1848, about 4,000 of California's 6,000 miners were Indians, working for themselves or for whites. Within months, however, their numbers began to drop, primarily as a result of fierce competition from the so-called forty-niners who were entering California in droves. More than 40,000 fortune hunters arrived in 1849 to stake claims in gold country. Mostly they were young, unattached males, sometimes of dubious background, and possessed of but a single thought: to get rich quick and return home in glory. In their eyes, Indians were competitors for the wealth, to be swept aside as swiftly as possible. Compounding this resentment was the visceral fear of the so-called wild Indian. As one prospector wrote of this supposed nemesis, "When you are in a country where you know he is your enemy, and is not only waiting his chance but looking out for his opportunity, why not cut him down as he most surely will you?"

As the forty-niners poured in, some large-scale operators began to hire them in place of Indians, in some cases because they feared retribution from whites. Indians working for themselves were often driven from the choicest spots and allowed to work only the tailings—material that had already been sifted through. Here and there, Indians held their own. At the southern fringe of gold country, the placers were not as rich. Whites there remained a minority for some time and had to reach an accommodation with the local villagers.

Elsewhere, however, violence erupted as intruders by the thousands not only deprived Indians of a livelihood but also menaced their communities. In March of 1849, a group of prospectors from Oregon invaded a Nisenan village near the Middle Fork of the American River, raped a number of women, and shot to death some of the men who fought back. A short time later, five miners on the Middle Fork were killed in apparent retaliation by an unknown party of Indians. Enraged, a band of 20 Oregonians descended on another Indian village, situated along Weber's Creek not far from Sutter's Mill. The attackers killed several dozen villagers and escorted a number of prisoners off to Sutter's Mill. There the Oregon men consumed a quantity of whiskey and proceeded to gun down seven of their captives, as if for sport, after first prodding them into running for their lives. The victims, it turned out, had been employed at the mill and almost certainly had nothing to do with the killing of the white men. As word spread of the Weber Creek massacre, a large number of Indians who were still sifting for gold left the mining sites and returned to their villages. Charles Weber and his partners found themselves virtually abandoned by their large force of Yokuts in the wake of the attack.

Soon the violence bred by the frantic pursuit of riches spread to other areas of California. Later in 1849, Pomo Indians at Clear Lake, some 80 miles north of San Francisco, rose up against two particularly oppressive masters, ranchers Andrew Kelsey and a man known only as Stone, who had recently joined in the gold rush. The two Anglos had taken 27 Pomos to the diggings, where they quickly amassed a huge sack of gold—for which each Indian received a pair of overalls, a shirt, and a handkerchief. Kelsey and Stone invested their profits in 1,000 head of cattle. Those animals overgrazed the area, consuming the seed-bearing grasses and driving out the game the Indians depended on. The two partners not only stinted on food for their laborers but whipped them for little or no reason and further antagonized them by seizing the Indian wife of a ranch hand named Augustin. At last, the Pomos acted to rid themselves of their tormentors. One night Augustin's wife, who was being held in the house, fouled her captors' weapons by pouring water down the barrels. The next morning, the Indians cornered Kelsey and Stone and did away with them.

Retribution came swiftly in the form of a U.S. Army detachment, dispatched to the scene along with a gang of civilian volunteers. They found the Pomos encamped along Clear Lake. "The troops came unexpectedly upon a body of Indians numbering between two and three hundred," reported San Francisco's *Daily Alta California,* one of several newspapers in the state that did not shrink from detailing outrages by whites against Indians. "They immediately surrounded them, and as the Indians raised a shout of defiance and attempted to escape, poured a destructive fire indiscriminately upon men, women, and children."

The Indians preserved a somewhat different account of the massacre. By their own telling, the Pomos raised no howl of defiance, but came forward in peace and attempted to parley. A spokesman named Ge-Wii-Lih threw up his hands and said in broken English that he meant no harm. In response, a white man opened fire and wounded him in the arm, touching off a wholesale slaughter. One old Pomo woman looked on in horror as two whites impaled a little girl on the bayonets of their guns and tossed the body in the water. The same witness saw a little boy and a mother and baby put to death in similar fashion. One man was strung up by a noose, "and a large fire built under him," she added. "Another was tied to a tree and burnt to death." The army confirmed that 60 Indians were slain at Clear Lake, while another 75 died in a similar assault on a native village at the Russian River nearby.

As the Clear Lake Pomos had discovered to their dismay, the flood of

Indians caught up in the tumult of the gold rush trudge down a path, followed by a miner with a pickax protruding from his saddlebag, in an engraving of the period. At right, mining equipment is carried uphill by Chinese immigrants, who shouldered menial tasks for prospectors as tensions mounted between whites and Indians.

prospectors and other intruders imperiled not only the people but also the land that sustained them. Sawmills and mining operations fouled the rivers and creeks to such an extent that fewer and fewer salmon swam up from the sea each year to spawn. Miners and settlers overran oak groves and relegated to their hogs the acorns that were the Indians' staff of life. Cattle and horses ate the grasses from which villagers harvested seeds. Fenced-in pastures and farmland ended the communal drives that once yielded large quantities of rabbits and ground squirrels. And larger game such as deer and elk scattered or fell before the relentless Anglo advance.

Unable to sustain themselves in traditional ways and barred from mining, many Indians emulated the mission fugitives of earlier days and resorted to raiding cattle and other livestock from miners living in the hills and ranchers in the valleys. The newspapers were filled with reports that reflected the Indians' plight. In Mendocino County, reported one journal, a rancher named Woodman "lost 109 horses, of which 74 were found dead, upon the bodies of which the Indians were having a good feast." The desperation that drove Indians to such measures elicited little sympathy from miners and ranchers, many of whom reacted in fury to the mere suspicion of stock theft. In the spring of 1850 on the Middle Fork of the Feather River, a group of goldminers found several head of oxen missing and assumed that Indians had stolen the animals. A gang of 15 men proceeded to a village 12 miles up in the mountains, where they found a few bones lying about. With no more proof than that, the miners murdered 14 Indians and razed the village. Upon their return home, the avengers were in for a surprise. Approaching camp, they discovered the missing oxen grazing placidly in a canyon, where they had wandered in search of grass.

The confrontations grew increasingly bloody. On October 25, 1850, California's governor ordered an expedition by 200 militiamen against Indian raiders on the North Fork of the Consumnes River, in Miwok territory. Finding some freshly butchered cattle, the militiamen pressed on a few more miles and encountered about 200 Miwoks, fully prepared to defend themselves. They may not all have been raiders, but they knew that the whites considered them enemies to the last man, and they expected no mercy. A chaotic battle ensued along the rim of the canyon, where the terrain made it difficult for the militiamen to profit from their firearms; some combatants grappled hand to hand and tumbled down the steep slopes. Three Indians were slain, but so fierce was the resistance that the whites were forced to retreat. Six days later, the militiamen fought another battle with 150 Miwoks, some of them armed with shotguns and rifles. Fifteen Indians and two whites were killed before the contest ended and the militiamen called off their expedition. The toll had been steep for the Miwok warriors, but they may well have averted the annihilation of their band.

T
he Indians who lived in central California bore the brunt of the pressure from intruders during the gold rush years. But wherever the Anglo-Americans went, they raised fears among native peoples by virtue of their sheer numbers and their determination to subdue the land and its inhabitants. In the south, their presence stirred an Indian revolt just months after California was admitted to the Union in September of 1850. The leader of the uprising was Antonio Garra, a former mission neophyte who headed the Cupeño. Longtime neighbors of the Cahuilla, the Cupeño lived in the semiarid hill country south of Palm Springs. Franciscan friars had established mission outposts there in the early 1800s and introduced Christianity, cattle, and a few crops. After the secularization of the missions, a large chunk of Cupeño territory had been claimed first by the Mexican rancher José Pico and later by an Anglo-American who adopted Spanish ways and took the name Juan José Warner. The Cupeño resented the arrogant Warner, who, as one visitor put it,

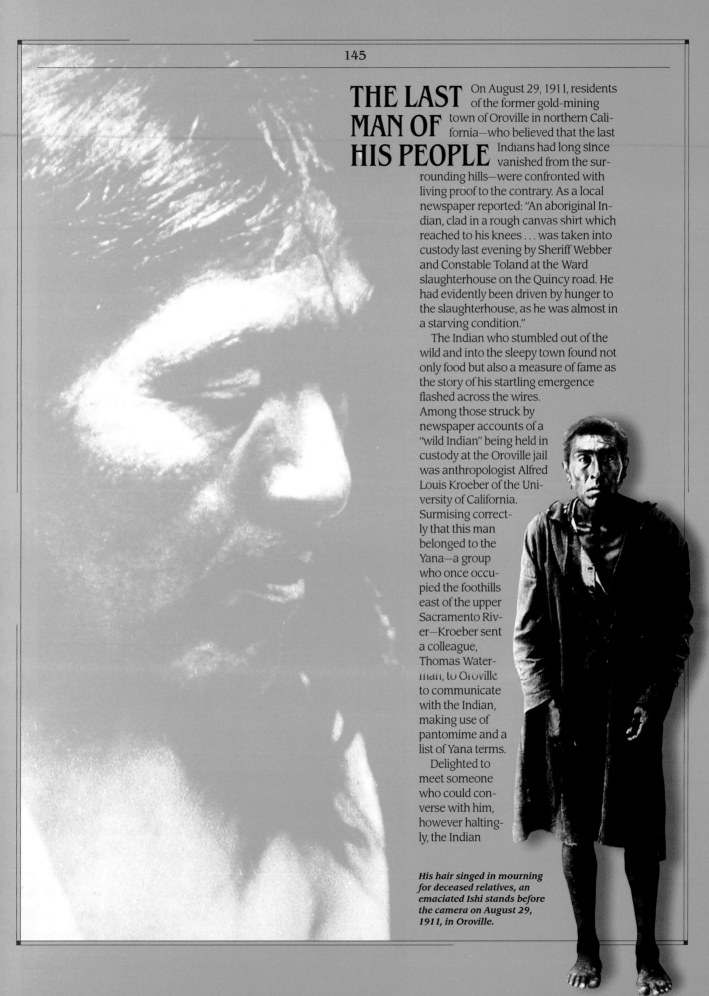

THE LAST MAN OF HIS PEOPLE

On August 29, 1911, residents of the former gold-mining town of Oroville in northern California—who believed that the last Indians had long since vanished from the surrounding hills—were confronted with living proof to the contrary. As a local newspaper reported: "An aboriginal Indian, clad in a rough canvas shirt which reached to his knees ... was taken into custody last evening by Sheriff Webber and Constable Toland at the Ward slaughterhouse on the Quincy road. He had evidently been driven by hunger to the slaughterhouse, as he was almost in a starving condition."

The Indian who stumbled out of the wild and into the sleepy town found not only food but also a measure of fame as the story of his startling emergence flashed across the wires. Among those struck by newspaper accounts of a "wild Indian" being held in custody at the Oroville jail was anthropologist Alfred Louis Kroeber of the University of California. Surmising correctly that this man belonged to the Yana—a group who once occupied the foothills east of the upper Sacramento River—Kroeber sent a colleague, Thomas Waterman, to Oroville to communicate with the Indian, making use of pantomime and a list of Yana terms.

Delighted to meet someone who could converse with him, however haltingly, the Indian

His hair singed in mourning for deceased relatives, an emaciated Ishi stands before the camera on August 29, 1911, in Oroville.

During a visit to Yahi territory in 1914, Ishi draws his bow.

agreed to travel to San Francisco as a guest of the anthropologists. They confirmed that he was a Yahi, the southernmost of four small bands constituting the Yana. When asked his name, however, he remained silent, for in his culture that was too personal a matter to reveal. Kroeber dubbed him Ishi, a word from the Yahi dialect meaning "person," or "one of the people." In fact, he was one of only a few dozen Yanas left—and the last of the Yahis.

When the gold rush began, there had been as many as 2,000 Yanas living in the foothills. Their territory was serrated by steep ridges and deep gorges and covered with dense brush, pines, and oaks. In this rugged setting, the Yana subsisted by fishing, hunting, and gathering acorns.

This way of life was imperiled by the sudden influx of miners and ranchers about 1850. The intruders' livestock devoured nourishing acorns and seeds, and hunters killed or drove off much of the game. The Yana could survive only by raiding the ranches and farms that were sprouting up in their territory. White vigilantes struck back, slaughtering scores of Yanas at a time. By 1872 the Yahis were reduced to an isolated group of five, including Ishi—who was about 10 years old at the time—his mother, and his sister. When he came down from the mountains in 1911, he was the last of his people.

Despite his long, lonely ordeal, Ishi adapted to his strange new surroundings with poise and grace. He lived at the University of California's Museum of Anthropology in San Francisco, occupying the guest quarters there and earning his keep as a caretaker. At other times, he imparted Yahi language and ways to the anthropologists or demonstrated traditional crafts to visitors. To satisfy the public's curiosity, he agreed to demonstrate his skills on Sunday afternoons. At first, the crowds that flocked to see him frightened Ishi, who had seldom been surrounded by more than a few people. But he soon grew accustomed to the attention and calmly demonstrated to onlookers how to chip an arrowhead or carve a bow. He even built a Yahi thatched summer dwelling on the museum grounds.

Ishi sits proudly before a Yana house he built on the museum grounds.

Crafting a salmon harpoon like the one at right, Ishi lashes wooden prongs to a pole.

Ishi adopted many of the ways of his hosts, not because he considered them superior but because that was the polite thing for a guest to do in his culture. He readily donned jacket, shirt, and trousers, but he deemed shoes too stiff, tolerating them only in winter. He was not content simply to help Kroeber understand and transcribe the Yahi dialect. Ishi himself wrestled with English. Although his pride prevented him from saying an English word until he was sure of its pronunciation and meaning, he often tactfully mispronounced Yahi words the way whites did so as not to embarrass them.

Those who got to know Ishi found him a warm companion. Yet he remained aware of his distinct identity. Kroeber's wife, Theodora, who told Ishi's story in writing, paraphrased his attitude: "I am one; you are others; this is in the inevitable nature of things."

In the spring of 1914, Ishi joined Kroeber, Waterman, surgeon Saxton Pope, and Pope's son on a trip to Yahi territory. For the scientists, this was a long-awaited chance to see Ishi in his element and document his world in words and pictures. For Ishi, however, the trip meant a return to a landscape fraught with danger—a place where his kinspeople had died and where their spirits might still linger. The Yahi believed that unless the dead were properly cremated, their spirits might wander and endanger the living. Ishi's family had lived on the run. His sister, for one, had disappeared, and he never had the opportunity to lay her to rest.

On the first night of the trip, while the other men slept, Ishi went off into the woods. He returned before dawn and

Ishi butchers a deer in the traditional way. He made the knife above from bottle glass during his years in hiding.

remarked to Pope's son: "It is good. None are lost. They found their way."

His mind unburdened, he guided his friends through his territory, pointing out a favorite fishing spot, the site of a former village, the place where he had killed a bear. Instead of struggling to explain himself verbally, he was now free to demonstrate how the Yahi hunted and fished. He had no desire to remain in the land of his ancestors, however. After a few weeks had passed, he was ready to return to the museum, the place he now called home.

Late that year, Ishi developed the first symptoms of tuberculosis, and his condition soon worsened. On March 25, 1916, he died at the museum. Kroeber advised against an autopsy, knowing that it was Ishi's wish to reach his spiritual home intact. But Saxton Pope invoked the interests of science: An autopsy was performed, and Ishi's brain was preserved. His remains were then cremated along with traditional objects that Ishi had crafted or collected, including a bow, arrows, flakes of obsidian, a pouch of tobacco, shell beads used by the Yahi as money, and a basket of acorn meal. More than all the tributes from his friends, the funeral offerings told of Ishi's legacy—patient efforts that helped to preserve the lore of his people and show that the "last wild Indian," as some called him, was in fact the product of an accomplished native society.

Ishi and a Yana man, Sam Batwi, attend a vaudeville show with Alfred Kroeber (back row, second from left) and others.

Shown here in 1911, Ishi begins a new life.

kept his Indian laborers "in a sort of serfdom." The seething discontent around Warner's Ranch helped fuel Garra's revolt.

Antonio Garra had not always been a foe of the Americans. Indeed he had previously made overtures to American officers during their war with the Mexicans in the hope of improving the lot of his people. Garra, acknowledged the *San Diego Herald* after that conflict, "is regarded by all who know him as a man of energy, determination, and bravery. His power and influence among the Indians is almost unbounded." Yet by 1851, this esteemed and once-friendly leader had concluded that the Americans must be driven from California. The immediate cause of his wrath was an onerous local tax imposed on property that the Indians had managed to retain despite the maneuvers of ranchers like Pico and Warner. The levy might have been tolerable if the Anglo-Americans had extended to the native peoples the rights that went along with duties such as taxation. Instead the new masters of California seemed bent on depriving Indians of any power that remained to them. "If we lose this war," Garra told a fellow chief, "all will be lost—the world. If we gain this war, then it is forever; never will it stop; this war is for a whole life."

Garra hoped to enlist other southern tribal groups in his cause, including the nearby Cahuilla, Luiseño, and Kumeyaay, and the Quechan and Cocopa along the Colorado River. His plan was first to capture Camp Independence, a U.S. Army outpost charged with guarding a key ferry crossing on the Colorado. Then, with that choke point in their possession, the allies would descend in a coordinated attack upon San Diego, Santa Barbara, Los Angeles, and other non-Indian settlements in the south. Mexicans would be spared; only the Anglos would be killed. Since there was little gold in the south and the American presence was still relatively modest, victory seemed possible.

But Garra, for all his influence and determination, could not convince many of his would-be allies that the Americans posed a fatal threat. Some Indian groups decided to remain on good terms with the newcomers. Garra went ahead with only limited support. On November 10 at the Colorado River, his followers killed five sheepherders and took 1,500 sheep, but abandoned their goal of capturing Camp Independence—the place was stoutly defended by a howitzer and a detachment of troops. At Warner's Ranch a few days later, other Cupeños led by Garra's son joined with some sympathetic Cahuillas in an assault that left the ranch in flames and claimed the lives of four Americans in a nearby village. Yet the projected attacks on San Diego, Santa Barbara, and Los Angeles never materialized.

Antonio Garra himself met a bitter fate. In December he was lured to a meeting by Juan Antonio, chief of the Cahuilla, who had previously disassociated himself from the uprising. Juan Antonio seized Garra and turned him over to the U.S. Army. Charged with treason by a military tribunal, Garra responded through his defense counsel that he had never sworn allegiance to the United States. The court dropped that charge, but swiftly convicted Garra of theft and murder and sentenced him to death.

At his execution, a priest pleaded with the chief to seek forgiveness for his sins. According to a reporter who was on hand, Garra responded proudly, "Gentlemen, I ask your pardon for all my offenses, and expect yours in return." Then he knelt by his grave, and an officer shot him in the back of the head.

By his own admission, Garra never commanded more than 30 or 40 armed men during the course of the uprising. But the Anglos thought he had many more and that only his capture had prevented a bloodbath. Shortly after the Colorado River attack, the *Los Angeles Star* had reported that the Indians had overrun Camp Independence, slain all Americans in the area, and captured the fort's howitzer. On November 23, Mormon pioneers at San Bernardino had heard that Indians had razed Los Angeles. And on the 30th of the month, the general commanding the state militia had advised that if the Colorado River Indians ever linked up with those farther west, they would present a "force of four or five thousand

Militiamen fire on a Yuki village in Mendocino County in the late 1850s as part of a ruthless campaign to punish poachers and sweep Indians from their land. Assaults and disease cut the Yuki population from more than 6,000 in 1850 to barely 300 in 1864.

warriors. It would strain the energies of the country to their utmost tension, to resist so formidable a combination, if it could be resisted at all."

All of this was soon shown to be nonsense. But the frightful vision of Indian hordes persisted, and dozens of volunteer companies rallied to suppress the presumed threat—all at state expense. When Garra's uprising collapsed, the volunteers sought other targets, seldom bothering to establish whether the Indians they went after were indeed hostile. In 1851 and 1852, the California legislature authorized payment of $1.1 million to reimburse citizens for "private military forays."

Meanwhile, federal commissioners from Washington were trying to resolve California's "Indian problem" and bring a semblance of order to the nation's newest and potentially richest state. Shortly after California's admission to the Union, three federal Indian commissioners arrived to assess the situation. The commissioners put it bluntly to state authorities: As there was "no further west" to which Indians could be removed, there appeared to be only two alternatives: "extermination or domestication."

To their credit, the commissioners ruled out the first option and spent more than a year negotiating 18 treaties with various bands. All told, only about 25,000 Indians were involved, or no more than one-fifth of the state's native population. When it came time to negotiate a treaty, the officials simply met with groups of Indians where they found them, explained the treaty as best they could, and asked leaders for signatures. Although an interpreter was usually present, he was often unfamiliar with the local Indian languages and dialects. Nevertheless, the commissioners managed to collect endorsements.

By these treaties, the Indians agreed to acknowledge American sovereignty over all land ceded to the United States by Mexico in 1848 and to refrain from hostilities against U.S. citizens. In return, the United States agreed to set aside for their exclusive use 7,488,000 acres, or 7.5 percent of the state's area, in 18 parcels running up the center of California. The Indians were promised ample food, clothing, livestock, and tools, along with assistance from farmers, blacksmiths, wheelwrights, schoolteachers, and others. Commissioner George Barbour wrote to his superior in Washington after signing one treaty in May 1852: "You will probably think the amount agreed to be given to those tribes with whom we have treated too great; but when you take into consideration their poverty, the country they surrender, and particularly the expense of a war with them that would necessarily last for years, to say nothing of the gold mines they give up, I do not think you will conceive that we have given them too much."

Representatives of several northern California peoples gather in 1858 with Indian agents (standing at far left) after agreeing to the establishment of the Round Valley Reservation. Set up as a federal farm for Indians, Round Valley forced surviving Yukis together with Nomlakis, Maidus, and Pomos.

Most white Californians were outraged. They conceded that there were some "useful" Indians living in the state—which was to say, former mission Indians who toiled as laborers on farms and ranches. These could be left alone. But the rest were a "source of much annoyance," as Governor John McDougal put it, and must be removed "to some isolated position distant from all contact with the whites." Some citizens demanded that the native Californians be removed east to the sparsely occupied Great Basin; others seriously proposed that they be dumped on either San Pedro or Santa Catalina Islands, off the southern California coast. Few whites were in any mood to relinquish good land to the Indians. Such pressure did the Anglos apply that the U.S. Senate in June 1852 rejected the treaties. Some Indians had already given up their homelands in exchange for territories promised by treaty. Now they had nothing.

The relocation policy that finally emerged from Washington was satisfactory to no one. Instead of being offered treaty lands of their own, the so-called wild Indians were to be resettled on federal land. There, under the watchful eye of American troops and an agent from the Bureau of Indian Affairs, they would be provided with rations and taught farming. Those who made the difficult transition would have no legal claim to the land and could be relocated at any time.

Between 1853 and 1860, seven of these so-called farms were established. Three were in south-central California—Tejon Pass, at the lower end of the San Joaquin Valley; Tule River, in the foothills at the southern edge of the Sierras; and Fresno River, within the territory of the Northern Valley Yokuts. The other four were in the northwest—Nome Lackee, so called for the Nomlaki who lived around the site, between the Coast Ranges and the Sacramento Valley; Round Valley, in Yuki territory to the west, near the Eel River; Mendocino, near present-day Fort Bragg; and Klamath River, in Yurok territory to the north.

None of these farms flourished. Not only were many Indians relocated there unwillingly, but a single site often housed members of different bands or tribal groups. At best, those factions had trouble communicating; at worst, they were outright enemies. Living among strangers was anathema to most Indians under any circumstances. One Kumeyaay woman later explained why her family fled to Mexico rather than settle with other Indians at the behest of the government: "In those days when you were with one group, you stick with that group. You can't go in with another."

The farms, which were limited to 25,000 acres, offered generally poor prospects for farming, but that did not keep ranchers and other ambitious whites from encroaching on them and threatening the Indian occupants. The promised tools and agricultural instruction were either late or not forthcoming at all, and medical attention was scant. To make matters worse, some of the agents defrauded their charges by selling to miners and other whites the government beef meant for hungry Indians. Even the honest agents lacked much understanding of the people they supervised. At Tejon Pass, for example, where hundreds of former mission Indians had been getting by for some time as subsistence farmers, the agent revived bitter memories by introducing a compulsory labor system. "If I were to allow them to work when they pleased," he insisted, "but little would be

Hupas await the distribution of government rations at their Hoopa Valley Reservation, established in 1864. Although Hupas won the right to remain here on their ancestral territory by waging war against white encroachment, they suffered under federal supervision: One corrupt agent increased their dependence on rations by allowing whites to harvest Indian grain and purchase government farm equipment for a pittance.

done, for the industrious would be discouraged by the indolent; but as it is, the indolent are punished and compelled to labor." Although his method helped to produce a surplus of crops, it alienated the Indians, who would have been content to meet their needs while retaining their dignity.

At Fresno River, Yokuts regularly hunted wild horses to supplement their meager diet, while at Klamath River, the determined Yuroks flatly refused to engage in agriculture, saying that if the white man would just leave them alone, they could make do as their ancestors had. At Nome Lackee, crop failures resulted in 25,000 fertile acres producing fewer than 12,000 bushels of grain. To supplement the poor yield, agents sent most of the 2,500 occupants out to harvest berries, acorns, grass seed, small game, and other natural bounty that had sustained them for centuries. But now there were whites living in the area who resented the proximity of Indians and felt that they could make better use of the land. Unchecked by authorities, they crowded in on the farm and eventually took it over. In 1863 the displaced Indians were escorted to Round Valley, where the Nomlaki found themselves hemmed in by white squatters and pressed together with Yuki Indians whom they had long considered enemies.

By this time, federal officials were rethinking their policies. Instead of becoming self-sufficient entities, one investigator reported, the farms "were simply Government almshouses where an inconsiderable number of Indians are insufficiently fed and scantily clothed, at an expense wholly disproportionate to the benefits conferred." Many disaffected Indians fled the farms, and most of the places went out of existence. Two of the original seven, Tule River and Round Valley, endured as part of an emerging network of federal reservations in California, some of which were considerably larger than 25,000 acres and all of which were supposed to remain free from encroachment. In most respects, however, the new reservations sprouting up around the state inherited the problems of their predecessors, including mismanagement, shortages of provisions, and tensions between rival Indian groups brought together at a single site.

Nothing the federal government did put an end to the murderous assaults on Indians. Indeed the creation of farms or reservations provided whites with a pretext for conducting savage roundups of native peoples. In many parts of California, especially in isolated mountain communities, Indians refused to abandon their ancient homelands for the vicissitudes of reservation life. Those holdouts often became targets for companies of local militiamen and volunteers. Typically they would surround an Indian village in the night and, with the coming of dawn, launch a brief, devastat-

ing assault, cutting down men, women, and children as they poured from their homes. The attackers would then round up the terrified survivors and march them off to the reservation, making sure to raze the village and destroy its food stocks before they left. The marauding companies often killed as many Indians as they collected.

The militiamen and volunteers claimed that in herding Indians onto reservations, they were simply enforcing government policy. But their prime motivation was hatred and fear of the Indians, who by that time were growing ever more desperate. Raids by native peoples on livestock persisted as hunger spread from village to village, and from time to time, Indians attacked intruders—assaults that were sometimes inflated in the telling and frequently prompted fierce retribution against the Indians. "The savages are paralyzing our best interests," wrote one aggrieved settler

Wintu men from the McCloud River area appear in war-dance outfits in a photograph from the late 1800s after many of their people were massacred or driven onto distant reservations. Despite assaults by encroaching whites—who on one occasion staged a "friendship feast" and poisoned 100 Wintus—some tribe members held out in their homeland until dams were built there in the 20th century, flooding their communities.

with more passion than truth. "Already they have destroyed all our grazing ground, and have driven the settlers from their homes; they have killed their stock, and daily commit outrages."

Another white Californian told of coming across the remains of an emigrant train in northeastern California that had been ambushed by Indians and witnessing the "naked bodies of murdered men, women, and children lying about in all directions among the charred wagons. The sight was indescribably horrible, and made every man clench his hands and set his teeth hard with a half-muttered vow of vengeance." The same man related how he and his armed companions then vented their rage on a nearby village that he claimed was home to more than 600 Indians: "We immediately charged them, shooting down men, squaws, and papooses indiscriminately. The slaughter—for it could hardly be called a fight—was over in half an hour, and we figured that scarcely 50 of the mob escaped; the rest were dispatched to the 'happy hunting ground' without the slightest show of mercy, and the poor emigrants were fearfully avenged."

Like the accounts of native atrocities, such tales of revenge were sometimes exaggerated, for men took a perverse pleasure in boasting of how many Indians they had killed. Yet the carnage was truly terrible. By conservative estimates, some 5,000 California Indians were killed by whites between 1848 and 1860. The toll may well have been higher, and the killing went on for another decade and more.

Some communities managed to survive only by retreating into country so rugged that hostile whites could not find them. In northern California, for example, a small band of Yana Indians called the Yahi fled into virtually impenetrable canyon country near Mount Lassen to evade further assaults by white vigilantes who were murdering their people to repay the killing of livestock. Amid the rigors of their new environment, their numbers dwindled. The last of the Yahis, Ishi, emerged from isolation in 1911 and did much to preserve the record of a people whose trials and accomplishments might otherwise have been lost to history.

Some other groups in northern California resisted attempts by whites to alienate them from their homelands. The most determined campaign was launched in 1872 by a band of Modocs, who eight years earlier had been driven from their ancestral land on California's northeastern plateau and forced onto the reservation of the Klamath Indians in southern Oregon. The conditions they encountered there were discouraging in the extreme. Food was scarce, and what there was went mainly to the Klamath, who outnumbered them. Fiercely independent, the Modocs yearned to regain control of their destiny. In April 1870, about 150 men, women, and children under the leadership of Keintpoos—or Captain Jack, as he was known to some—fled the reservation and returned to their homeland around Tule Lake. There they drew inspiration from the Ghost Dance, a ceremony that originated among the Paiute of the Great Basin, whose shamans promised that all dead Indians would soon return from the spirit world to reclaim their homelands. A visiting shaman named Doctor George brought the word to the Modocs at Tule Lake in the winter of 1871. "He said the dead would come from the east when the grass was about eight inches high," reported one Ghost Dancer. "The deer and the animals were all coming back, too. The whites were to burn up and disappear without even leaving ashes."

The ghosts did not return with the growing grass, and the excitement subsided. But Captain Jack was determined that he and his people would keep faith with their ancestors by remaining free. When white authorities came to parley with him that summer, he refused to lead a return to the Klamath Reservation. In November 1872, a detachment of cavalry rode out to capture the Modocs and collided with Captain Jack's well-armed men; eight soldiers and 15 Indians were killed or wounded in the fight. Captain Jack and his people executed a fighting retreat to a massive lava bed on the south shore of Tule Lake. Although seemingly inhospitable, the terrain was riddled with caves that offered the Modocs shelter and was covered with sagebrush and greasewood that provided fuel. In mid-January of 1873, the army sent 400 men with artillery support to pry the Modocs from their stronghold. An all-day fight ensued among the rocks before the troops retreated with nine dead and 30 wounded.

After biding their time, the authorities sought further negotiations. A meeting was arranged for April 11. Some warriors among the Modocs argued that whites could never be trusted and proposed killing the peace commissioners. Captain Jack believed that such a deed would bring the full fury of the U.S. Army down upon the Modocs. Goaded by the militants, however, he decided to go along with their scheme rather than abandon them to it. At the meeting, he and five of his warriors suddenly drew pistols from their robes and started shooting: General Edward Canby and another white negotiator fell dead. Amid the confusion, Captain Jack escaped. On April 26, he and his band ambushed an army search party in the lava beds, killing 26 soldiers and wounding 16.

The massive show of force that Captain Jack had feared soon materialized. In May the army brought up 1,000 troops, assisted by Indian re-

The lava beds south of Tule Lake offered cover to the Modocs led by Captain Jack after they fled the Klamath Reservation and returned to their homeland. Army troops went after them in 1872, helped by Indian recruits including men from the Warm Springs Reservation (shown amid the lava beds below).

cruits. Step by step, the soldiers started to penetrate the Indians' natural fortress. On May 22, a small party of Modocs gave up. On June 1, Captain Jack and his remaining 50 warriors surrendered, along with the women and children. Although the conflict would be remembered later as the Modoc War, Captain Jack and his chief lieutenants were treated as criminals and executed by hanging on October 3, 1873. The remnants of his band were deported to the Indian Territory, located in present-day Oklahoma, where they and their descendants remained until 1909, when they were allowed to rejoin the few remaining Modocs on the Klamath Reservation that Captain Jack had fought so hard to avoid.

By the time Captain Jack's Modocs surrendered in 1873, the shooting war against California's Indians—most of it carried out by state militiamen, volunteers, and vigilantes—had largely subsided. Indian resistance had been all but extinguished. Yet the militiamen and their ilk could not claim all the credit for eradicating a way of life. From the start, assaults of a different nature had been made against native peoples and their culture, some of them even more demoralizing than the armed forays.

Although many white Californians in isolated mining and ranching areas wanted nothing to do with Indians, others saw a use for them as servants or slaves. Technically, slavery was illegal in the state of California from its inception, but between 1850 and 1863, state legislators enacted a series of provisions that skirted the prohibition. One denied Indians the right to testify in court, thereby eliminating any protection they might enjoy under the state and federal constitutions. It read in part: "In no case shall a white man be convicted of any offense upon the testimony of an Indian." A second provision decreed that any Indian, merely upon the word of a white person, could be declared a "vagrant." Thereafter he or she could be auctioned off to the highest bidder for a period of labor not to exceed four months. More baneful still, under the law, any white person desiring the services of an Indian child—boys under 18, girls under 15—had only to appear before a justice of the peace with the "child's parents or friends." If the justice agreed that no coercion was involved, he could issue a certificate authorizing that person

Encamped along Tule Lake, army troops and Indian recruits kept pressure on the Modocs during negotiations. The talks, aided by interpreters Frank Riddle and his Modoc wife, Winema (top right and center), ended violently when the Modocs chose to fight rather than return to the Klamath Reservation. As Captain Jack said, "Kill with bullet don't hurt much, starve to death hurt a heap."

to have the "care, custody, control, and earnings of such minor, until he or she obtain the age of majority."

Not all localities applied this statute, but some of those that did extended the age of majority far beyond the threshold at which whites obtained their full legal rights. In 1861 the *Sacramento Daily Union* published the names of 45 Indians bound over to a pair of ranchers in Tehama County: "Little Sam, 12, bound until 25; Fanny, 12, bound until 25; Nancy, 15, bound until 30; Jack White, 16, bound until 30." And so it went with Simon, Elijah, Ambrose, Myra, Maggie, Venus, and the rest.

This indenture system allowed whites to exploit Indian workers for many years at minimal expense, all behind a veil of legality. But law enforcement was lax in the early years of statehood, and other whites who coveted Indian labor simply took advantage of the illegal slave trade that flourished in California well into the 1860s. The practice of raiding Indian villages for laborers went back to Spanish colonial days. Now some Anglos began to specialize in the business of capturing Indians for sale, with children and young women being the main targets. It was far simpler to buy youngsters outright than to indenture them. In 1854 San Francisco's *Daily Alta California* reported that "abducting Indian children has become quite a common practice. Nearly all the children belonging to some of the Indian tribes in the northern part of the state have been stolen." When militiamen targeted an Indian village, it was no rare thing for the kidnappers to trail behind them in order to scoop up surviving children. The *Daily Alta California* in 1862 printed the report of a prospector named Hess, who had recently returned from the Sacramento basin: "In one instance, he saw two men driving nine children; in another, two men with four children; in another, one man with two girls, one of them about 14 years of age." Rumor had it that some of the slave hunters had obtained the children by killing their parents.

By one estimate, as many as 4,000 Indian children were kidnapped for the slave trade between 1850 and the years immediately following the Civil War, when the prohibition against slavery finally began to take hold in California. During that period, the prices offered for Indians made many a trader wealthy. According to one observer: "Indians seven or eight years old are worth $100. It is a damned poor Indian that's not worth $50." One slave owner was prepared to offer a "Spanish horse for a good little Digger." Whether indentured or enslaved, young Indians were usually assigned such household chores as carrying water, washing dishes and clothes, helping with the cooking, and playing nursemaid to their masters' younger children. Many masters professed fondness for these servants, but even an infraction as minor as an unauthorized visit home could trigger harsh punishment. The *San Francisco Bulletin* in 1860 told of a rancher it identified only as "L" whose Indian boy occasionally slipped away to visit relatives living within half a mile of the ranch. "This incensed L so much," wrote the *Bulletin,* "that he went down one morning and slaughtered the whole family—of about six persons—boy and all."

Women and girls often suffered the additional burden of sexual exploitation. Although white men often derided Indians as unattractive, quite a few of them purchased Indian women and kept them as servants and concubines. A girl considered suitable for those purposes could bring

After yielding to the army in June of 1873, Modoc warrior John Schonchin (far left) stands chained to Captain Jack, who sometimes wore a fringed buckskin shirt (near left). The two men were among four Modocs executed for killing federal negotiators.

$200 or more on the slave market in a state flooded with unattached males. Some white men who did not care to pay for permanent companionship felt free to rape Indian women. During the 1850s, California newspapers were filled with accounts of sexual assaults on Indians in the mining districts. One newspaper complained of men who, when they could not "obtain a squaw by fair means, would not hesitate to use foul." Indeed some of the Indian attacks that so provoked whites were retaliations for rape—a crime that native groups abhorred among themselves and were disposed to punish severely when perpetrated by whites. In one instance, when a Nisenan woman was raped and abducted by a miner named Big Tom, her people demanded her return. When Tom refused, a group of Nisenan warriors attacked his camp, rescued the woman, killed Tom's companions, and chopped the rapist himself into pieces.

Not all interracial unions were forced on Indian women or devoid of affection. Some native women welcomed relationships with white men who treated them kindly and shielded them from hunger and abuse. Many Anglos scorned the whites who entered into such relationships as "squaw men," however, and derided their offspring as half-breeds. Other Indian women turned to prostitution to survive—a desperate measure that the men of their band sometimes tacitly accepted or even encouraged. By 1856, one traveler reported, the Miwok in the Yosemite area were so demoralized that "many of their young women were used as commercial property and peddled out to the mining camps and gambling saloons." Their life was short and bitter. "In one or two years, they become diseased," wrote an official at the Fresno River Farm, "and at the age of 20 wear the features of 35 to 40; and as a general thing before they arrive at the age of 30, die a shameful and miserable death."

Many of the women contracted venereal diseases, which spread devastation among tribal groups of the interior as they had earlier among the coastal peoples. And numerous other ills were communicated to Indians by whites as they settled the state—including cholera, typhoid, malaria, smallpox, whooping cough, and measles. In 1849 villagers near Yuba City in the Sacramento Valley were struck by cholera; 100 of 500 Indians perished. In 1852 a smallpox epidemic struck around Nevada City, in the foothills to the east, and carried away one-fifth of the native population. A year later, 800 Indians in Butte County to the north died of pneumonia, influenza, and tuberculosis. Outbreaks such as these, combined with the attacks on Indians by whites, resulted in calamitous population declines. According to one estimate, about 7,000 Nisenans lived in and around gold country in 1850. By 1865 only some 1,600 remained. Their southern neighbors, the Miwok, reportedly lost more than half their population between 1850 and 1856. The number of Indians living in Sutter County plummeted from more than 500 in 1852 to just 10 in 1860. By that time, there were only about 32,000 Indians living in all of California—compared with at least 125,000 in 1848. By 1865 the number had dwindled to 23,000. It seemed to be only a matter of time before Indians vanished from a region that had supported one of the densest and most varied indigenous populations to be found anywhere in North America.

Although the plight of the Indians seemed hopeless, those who survived had one great thing in their favor—their intimate knowledge of the land and its resources, which enabled them to make a living in country that whites found unrewarding. One group of Cahuillas who were allotted a reservation on arid land in the San Jacinto Mountains managed quite well through this difficult period by channeling runoff to irrigate crops, by raising livestock, and by sending down teams each year to shear sheep for local whites. Far to the north, along the Russian River, a band of about 135 Pomos created their own homestead by scraping together $800 in 1881 to make a down payment on 120 acres of arable land. By selling their produce, making baskets, and working for neighboring whites, they eventually managed to pay off the remaining $3,700 mortgage and secure a firm title to their land. As time went by, some whites who dealt with such groups came to respect them—and even welcome them as neighbors.

Yet the pressures of an ever-expanding white population left native peoples little room for such quiet achievements. The majority of California Indians shunned reservations and tried to remain independent, but their struggle was often a lonely one, with little prospect of success. When villagers were driven from their land by white ranchers and farmers, communities frequently splintered, leaving families to fend for themselves. One Kumeyaay woman who crossed with her family into Mexico to avoid

An Indian woman and her white husband stand proudly with their children—including an infant cradled in a traditional baby basket—in a northwestern California village in the late 1800s. Some whites "have been honest enough to wed our women under their laws," explained Yurok Lucy Thompson, "and some of them have married under both the white man's and the Indian's marriage laws." The children from these unions, she added, "make men and women that the American nation might well be proud of."

being confined to a reservation struggled to support herself and her children through traditional methods. "Things got pretty bad," she recalled. "I went out on my own and gathered food. I had been taught all these things about how to gather and prepare wild food. I went out and hunted for wild greens and honey. I took Aurelio and we hunted with his bow and arrows and his rabbit stick. Sometimes we found things. Lots of times we did not and we went hungry. I had to beg for food from neighboring Indians and ranchers." Other Indians moved to dismal camps on the outskirts of Anglo

AN ALBUM OF NATIVE EXILES

While vacationing in southern California in the late 1890s, Constance Goddard Du Bois, a romance novelist from Connecticut, came upon a story that was more compelling than fiction—the struggles of local Luiseño and Kumeyaay peoples to maintain slender footholds in their former homelands.

Moved by what she saw, Du Bois stayed in California and became an advocate for displaced Indians. Over the years, she traced their ordeal in an album of photographs, accompanied by her handwritten captions.

Some Indians in the area had been relegated to tiny reservations like Inaja *(lower right)*, where they strained to make a living; others had remained at old mission outposts like San Felipe *(left)*, only to be ousted by whites who claimed title to the land. Those exiled camped in the hills or built shelters on bleak spots such as Volcan Mountain. In documenting all this, the novelist brought to light a true tale of hardship and perseverance.

1901

Group of San Felipe Indians dressed in their best clothes to have their picture taken, perhaps the last time they will assemble by the chapel which cost them so much in gifts and labor. The greedy white men have coveted their few miserable acres to add to their own rich valley land, and the Indians are to be driven out away from their houses, chapel and all the improvements their hard labor has made in this barren spot.

Old Indians camping out to find work among white men — N. G. 1901

1897

Indian house on Santa Ysabel ranch
One of the few remaining houses of former
prosperous Indian village; soon
claimed by ranch owners and Indians
driven back on to Volcan Mt.

Men thrashing grain at Duaja.
They had hired a machine. They
can raise a little grain but nothing
else. 20 acres to 45 people.

1907

Manzanita reservation. Only eight acres of poor farming land in a reservation of rocks and sand for fifty-three people. S.M.B. 190

Is Foster's winter house at La Posta. Stony hill shows character of most of the reservation land. S.M.B. 1901

Peña's house foot of Volcan - Ranch company have moved their lines to include his house, garden & land.

Interior of Osuna's ramada - Summit of Volcan - He is the only Indian who has a good piece of land - He took possession before it was made a reservation and chose the only fertile spot -

Jo Foster's summer dwelling - ramada - His family - He is the most industrious Indian but has no land - Works at a distance for a white man -

S.M.B. 1901

towns and eked out a wretched existence as cheap seasonal labor for farmers and ranchers.

Most Indians on the reservations fared little better materially and had to put up with intrusive federal policies. At best, the reservations were sanctuaries for Indians in a hostile world. Some of them indeed helped preserve communities that might otherwise have ceased to exist. And the health services provided to reservation dwellers gradually improved and helped reverse the ruinous decline of the native population. But the agents and their superiors in Washington persisted in believing that they knew better than the Indians how to structure Indian lives—a confidence that was seldom borne out in the execution. Time and again, federal authorities imposed an ambitious scheme on the reservation dwellers, only to encounter obstacles and shift course, leaving Indians in the lurch.

Such basic questions as where to establish a reservation and who should reside there were resolved only with great difficulty by the government—and then in ways that alienated many Indians. After reservations were first proposed for the Luiseño in 1870, for example, it took five years to work out the particulars. Whites in the area, southeast of Los Angeles, opposed the idea of setting aside valuable land for Indians, while the Luiseño themselves split over the issue, with some favoring removal to reservations and others arguing that they should remain where they were no matter what the cost.

The plan implemented in 1875 was a poor compromise. A few Luiseño villages—including the one near an old mission site at Pala, northeast of San Diego—were allowed small reservations of their own. But other Luiseños were evicted from their homes and had to choose between moving to one of the reservations and taking their chances in the outside world. The transition was harrowing, and the reward for those who moved to Pala and settled down there was to discover a few decades later that the reservation did not really belong to the Luiseño after all. Henceforth they would have to share it with the Cupeño, who were ousted from their homes and escorted to Pala by government agents.

Ironically, the confinement of the Cupeño to the reservation at Pala came at a time when officials in Washington had shifted course and officially embraced the goal of assimilating reservation dwellers into white society. Much of the impetus for this campaign came from the General Allotment, or Dawes, Act, passed by Congress in 1887, which authorized the president to parcel out reservation land to Indian families or individuals, thus transforming them into private farmers or ranchers. In California, however, most of the reservations were judged too small or barren to be cut up into allotments that offered the Indians any chance of success. Four decades after the Dawes Act became law, only 11 of the 31 reservations in southern California had been allotted. Some California Indians living outside the reservations received allotments from the public domain or from land purchased by the federal government. Typically, several families settled on a bleak homesite that covered a few hundred acres at most. The place was called a *rancheria*—the old Spanish name for a small Indian village—but many of the homesites were communities in name only. The land was generally too poor to support the residents, and they then had to scrape for employment elsewhere.

Education was another instrument of assimilation that often had the effect of alienating California Indians. Beginning in the 1880s, the federal Bureau of Indian Affairs established 18 day schools and five boarding schools in and around reservations in California. Authorities had high hopes for the program, especially for the boarding schools, which were viewed as removing Indian children from what one administrator called the "corrupting and backward" influence of their parents. But the schools were a disaster from the start. Funding was so meager that only 20 cents a day was allocated for each student's food, not enough to meet the minimum requirements. Students and teachers had to perform most of the maintenance themselves, with the result that the turnover of teachers in the system approached 50 percent in some years. Discipline was harsh: A child caught speaking his native tongue instead of English, for example, might be beaten by his teacher. No less aggravating to students and their parents was the practice by schoolmasters of leasing out children in the boarding schools as domestics to white families nearby. Youngsters exploited in this way were sometimes prevented from visiting their own families during vacations.

Many Indians both on and off the reservation had little choice but to put up with the federal schools, for native children were long barred from public schools in California if there was a separate school for Indians in their district. Rather than subject their children to ill treatment, some parents simply kept them at home. In response, a few Indian agents resorted to coercion. In 1891 the agent in charge of the Hoopa Valley Reservation, along the northwest coast, went so far as to withhold the regular clothing issue from youngsters unless they attended the school there. Other officials persuaded concerned parents to send their children to distant boarding schools as a way of improving their prospects.

Elsie Allen, a Pomo Indian girl who lived in the vicinity of Santa Rosa, was 11 years old in 1910 when an agent talked her mother into sending her off to boarding school at Covelo, a town some 80 miles away. Until then, she had received no formal education whatsoever. Her memories of the school were bitter. "At that time, I could not yet speak English," she recalled, "and soon found myself unable to follow simple dressing and eating chores of the daily existence. They tried to keep me busy by giving me cards that had holes in them through which I was supposed to twist some yarn. It seemed so useless . . . I often cried at night with homesickness."

Not long after Elsie Allen arrived, the girls' dormitory was destroyed by a fire that she suspected was started by some of the older girls who had come to hate the school. It was not an isolated incident. Angry students or parents destroyed at least three other Indian schools, one of them at the Pachanga Reservation in the south, where in 1895 a Luiseño named Venturo Molido not only burned the building but also killed the teacher.

Wearing government-issue uniforms, Indian children assemble outside the federal boarding school that opened on the Hoopa Valley Reservation in 1893. A federal day school was established there earlier, but it proved so unpopular that it closed after a few years. To discourage resistance to the boarding school, government officials announced their intention to "compel the children to attend" by withholding disbursements of clothing from those who stayed away.

In time, Indians organized and demanded access to the public schools in their area. The state made a feeble attempt at integration in the early 1920s by partitioning classrooms and instructing Indian children separately. But half measures were not enough for one group of Pomos, who sued their local school board and won the right for their children to be educated alongside whites. In 1935 all restrictions on Indian enrollment in the state's public schools were removed.

The struggle for better schools was part of a larger effort by California's Indians to secure rights long denied to them. In the north, 3,000 people joined the Californian Indian Brotherhood, which campaigned not only for educational opportunities but also for tribal access to decent farmland. In the south, Indians banded together with sympathetic whites to form the Mission Indian Federation, which opposed any further allotment of reservation land by the federal government as an infringement on communal property rights. A leader on a reservation in the Palm Springs area spoke for many Cahuillas and other Indians in the region when he protested efforts in 1924 to survey reservation land and divide it into homesteads. "We were not notified and don't want allotments," he wired the secretary of the interior. "We have patent to our lands and want to hold them always together."

Although many California Indians welcomed access to public schools, they remained proud of their heritage and resented federal efforts to assimilate, or detribalize, them. Their complaints about the Bureau of Indian Affairs were echoed by native groups around the nation and ultimately were heard in Washington. In 1934 President Franklin Roosevelt extended his New Deal to reservation dwellers by appointing John Collier as commissioner of Indian affairs. A critic of detribalization, Collier prodded the U.S. Congress into passing the Indian Reorganization Act, which among

Indian horsemen, such as the vaqueros pictured here in 1920 on the sprawling Tejon Ranch south of Bakersfield, have served as expert cattle herders on California ranches since mission days. So respected were the Tejon vaqueros that the term "Indios del Tejon" became a title of honor.

Cahuillas from a nearby reservation prepare a meal for an event on the grounds of The Desert Inn at Palm Springs in 1915. Although many Cahuillas today live and work off their reservations, they value those communities as storehouses of tribal customs.

other things put an end to the allotment program and provided funds for land purchases to tribes that agreed to incorporate themselves and choose representatives to deal with the government. Although some tribal groups viewed this as meddling, 10 California reservations incorporated over the next several years and qualified for federal funds that they used to expand their communal holdings.

One thing that still rankled native Californians was the failure of the United States to honor the 18 treaties negotiated in 1852 but never ratified. Indians had been allowed to retain control of only a small fraction of the land promised them that year by federal commissioners. Nearly a century later, after lengthy litigation, a ruling in December 1944 awarded the California Indians $17.5 million for 7 million acres withheld from them. The government was allowed to deduct $12 million for its expenses on the Indians over the years, however. That left $5.4 million, or scarcely $150 apiece for the roughly 36,000 native Californians. Another lawsuit concerning the vast area of the state taken from Indians on other pretenses was settled in 1963 and resulted in the payment of $46 million to the state's Indian community for another 65 million acres.

Despite such acknowledgments of Indian rights, the federal government continued to sow discord by reviving detribalization after John Collier departed as commissioner in 1945. A policy known as termination called for the federal government to sever its ties with Indians and place them under state authority. As a result, California Indians lost federal health services they valued, and the state had to pick up the slack. In the end, however, protests from Indians and state officials blocked further federal efforts to allot reservation land to the individual occupants—a propos-

Some of the Indian activists from around the country who occupied Alcatraz Island in November 1969 gather at Indian Landing, as they dubbed the pier at the abandoned prison. In a mocking reference to the touted purchase of Manhattan Island from Indians for "trinkets," they offered to buy Alcatraz for 24 dollars in glass beads and red cloth.

al that most reservation dwellers continued to regard not as an entitlement but as a threat to their communities.

Another controversial aspect of the termination program was the effort to relocate Indians from reservations to urban areas, where they would presumably be assimilated. Under the program, as many as 50,000 Indians migrated to the Los Angeles and San Francisco areas from around the nation in the 1950s and 1960s. The process was disorienting both for the Indians who relocated and for native Californians of long standing, who found themselves outnumbered by the newcomers.

Yet differences between tribes became somewhat less of a barrier as Indians found common cause in their struggle for rights and recognition. California was the focus of one such demonstration of unity in November 1969, when some 300 activists calling themselves the Indians of All Tribes seized the abandoned federal prison on Alcatraz Island, citing a 100-year-old agreement by federal officials to allow nonreservation Indians to claim abandoned forts, prisons, and other obsolete government facilities.

Comparing Alcatraz to a reservation, the activists sent a Proclamation to the Great White Father, by which they promised to care for the island's fictional inhabitants—white people who could not fend for themselves. In this satirical document, the occupying Indians pledged to set up a Bureau of Caucasian Affairs that would hold the land in trust for the helpless whites. "We will further guide the inhabitants in the proper way of living," they promised. "We will offer them our religion, our education, our lifeways, in order to help them achieve our level of civilization and thus raise them, and all their white brothers up from their savage and unhappy state." The activists occupied Alcatraz for more than a year and a half, until the last of them were forcibly removed in June of 1971. Their determined protest not only drew the attention of whites to the shortcomings of federal Indian policies but became a source of pride for members of diverse tribes around the nation who were coming to identify themselves collectively as Native Americans.

For descendants of the first Californians, the spiritual and political revival of recent decades has meant honoring both their unique tribal heritage and the ties that bind them to other native peoples. Some teachers and elders around the state are working to preserve native languages. Although more than two dozen are still spoken in California, among some groups the number of people fluent in the ancestral tongue has dwindled to a mere handful. Loren Bommelyn, a schoolteacher in Crescent City on California's northwest coast, recently taught himself the language of his

Tolowa ancestors by working with the few elders who still spoke it. "How would you say this?" he asked them time and again. "How would you express this thought?" Eventually he gained sufficient command of the language to teach it to youngsters. At the far end of the state, meanwhile, the Cahuilla have been making similar efforts to preserve their language as they have other of their traditions.

In many places, native Californians have gone to great lengths to learn from their elders how to fashion the costumes and perform the dances that for centuries brought villagers together in celebration and thanksgiving. When members of different tribal groups gather today at festivals to perform their social dances for each other and for appreciative onlookers, they are helping in their way to renew the world, much as their ancestors did on sacred occasions.

That proud spirit of renewal was summed up by an Achumawi named Darryl Wilson when he and others of his group occupied part of northern California's Lassen Volcanic National Park, a few months after the Indians of All Tribes took over Alcatraz. There, on land once claimed by the Achumawi, they erected a shelter. Before long, authorities moved in, dismantled the building, and arrested 30 of the activists when they refused to go quietly. Darryl Wilson protested the action on behalf of his own people—and others like them around the nation, who were intent on reclaiming their heritage. According to Wilson, the authorities said the shelter was "ugly" and that it would have to be removed because it "ruined the landscape." But the Indians did not see it that way. "To us it was beautiful," Wilson said. "It was the beginning of our school. The meeting place. Home for our homeless. A sanctuary for those needing rest. Our church. Our headquarters. Our business office. Our symbol of approaching freedom."

Wearing the flicker-feather headband common to many tribes—and used as background on these pages—a dancer from the Grindstone Reservation, home of the Patwin and Nomlaki peoples, performs the traditional social dance called the Hoe-Down Dance.

INSPIRED BY DANCE

By the latter part of the 19th century, the native cultures of California had been pushed to the very brink of extinction. Nevertheless, the remnants of these hard-pressed tribal communities managed to preserve their treasured Indian heritage—inspired in no small part by the resurgence of their traditional Indian dances.

Functioning not only as an integral part of California Indian spirituality but also as a vital element of tribal life, dance expresses the relationship of native peoples with the earth and with nature, as well as with their creator and their fellow humans. Over the past century, age-old dances have helped some of the Indian communities to sustain their singular identity, in spite of efforts on the part of the federal government at forced assimilation.

In recent decades, interest and pride in the traditional ways have blossomed among native Californians. New groups have appeared to perpetuate both the ancestral dances and the splendid costumes associated with them. Events bringing together members of various tribal cultures such as Oakland's Festival at the Lake—scenes from which are featured here and on the following pages—have become increasingly popular. Central to these intertribal gatherings are performances of social dancing: festive displays that have ceremonial significance but at the same time are not too sacred to serve as entertainment for the participants and onlookers. By keeping up these rousing ceremonies, California Indians today seek not only to reaffirm their tribal ties but also to pass on the ancient traditions to new generations, thus ensuring that their culture will remain fresh and strong.

Singers from the Yurok tribe of northwest California provide accompaniment for the Brush Dance, which is traditionally performed by male Yuroks as part of a healing ceremony designed for children.

Originally held in anticipation of the coming of spring, the Maidu Toto Dance, like the Pomo Shakehead Dance, is performed by male (left) and female (above) dancers. Maidu women dancers move beaded belts up and down in rhythm with the accompaniment.

In the Sierra Miwok's lively Coyote Dance, the dancer who is designated the coyote—here the center man—disrupts his companions and tries to make them laugh. The dancers take great pride in the authenticity of their regalia. Said one tribal elder: "Nothing has been added, nothing taken away. And that's the way we want it to be."

Perched birdlike on one foot, two Chumash Indians follow the steps of their traditional Crane Dance. Native to the Santa Barbara area, the Chumash are known for their dances honoring the animal world, including the Blackbird Dance, the Dolphin Dance, and the Bear Dance.

ACKNOWLEDGMENTS

The editors wish to thank the following individuals and institutions for their valuable assistance in the preparation of this volume:

In Denmark: Copenhagen—Berete Due, Department of Ethnography, National Museum.
In Russia: Saint Petersburg—Konstantin Pozdnyakov, European House Publishers, Museum of Anthropology and Ethnography, Kunstkamera.
In the United States:

California: Berkeley—Lee Brumbaugh, Gene Prince, Phoebe A. Hearst Museum of Anthropology, University of California. Los Angeles—Ligia Perez, Kim Walters, Southwest Museum. Oakland—Carey Caldwell, Marcia Eymann, History Department, The Oakland Museum. Pala—Clifford "Tanty" Diaz, Cupa Cultural Center. Palm Springs—Kathy Clewell, Palm Springs Desert Museum; Cheryl Jeffrey, Agua Caliente Cultural Museum; Sally Hall McManus, Palm Springs Historical Society. Riverside—Chris L. Moser, Riverside Municipal Museum. Sacramento—Michael S. Tucker, California State Indian Museum.

San Diego—Jane Booth, Larry Booth, San Diego Historical Society; Ken Hedges, San Diego Museum of Man. San Marino—Jennifer Watts, The Huntington Library. Santa Barbara—Linda Agren, John Johnson, Santa Barbara Museum of Natural History. Stockton—Kat Anderson. Solvang—William S. Warwick, Old Mission Santa Ines. Ventura—Charles Johnson, Delee S. Marshall, Ventura County Museum of History and Art. Yosemite National Park—Craig D. Bates, The Yosemite Museum.
New Mexico: Santa Fe—Ralph Miguelena, Institute of American Indian Arts.

BIBLIOGRAPHY

BOOKS

Baer, Kurt, *The Treasures of Mission Santa Inés: A History and Catalog of the Paintings, Sculpture, and Craft Works.* Fresno: Academy of California Church History, 1956.

Bean, Lowell John, and Lisa J. Bourgeault, *The Cahuilla.* New York: Chelsea House Publishers, 1989.

Benson, Arlene, and Tom Hoskinson, eds., *Earth and Sky.* Thousand Oaks, Calif.: Slo'w Press, 1985.

Blackburn, Thomas C., ed., *December's Child: A Book of Chumash Oral Narratives.* Berkeley: University of California Press, 1975.

Blackburn, Thomas C., and Kat Anderson, eds., *Before the Wilderness: Environmental Management by Native Californians.* Menlo Park, Calif.: Ballena Press, 1993.

Boscana, Gerónimo, *Chinigchinich.* Rev. and ann. by John P. Harrington. Banning, Calif.: Malki Museum Press, 1978.

Brown, Vinson, and Douglas Andrews, *The Pomo Indians of California and Their Neighbors.* Ed. by Albert B. Elsasser. Happy Camp, Calif.: Naturegraph Publishers, 1990.

Carranco, Lynwood, and Estle Beard, *Genocide and Vendetta: The Round Valley Wars of Northern California.* Norman: University of Oklahoma Press, 1981.

Cook, Sherburne F., *The Conflict between the California Indian and White Civilization.* Berkeley: University of California Press, 1976.

Eargle, Dolan H., Jr., *The Earth Is Our Mother: A Guide to the Indians of California, Their Locales and Historic Sites.* San Francisco: Trees Company Press, 1992.

Emanuels, George, *California Indians: An Illustrated Guide.* Walnut Creek, Calif.: Diablo Books, 1991.

Engelhardt, Zephyrin, *San Diego Mission.* San Francisco: James H. Barry, 1920.

Erdoes, Richard, and Alfonso Ortiz, eds., *American Indian Myths and Legends.* New York: Pantheon Books, 1984.

Fleming, Paula Richardson, and Judith Luskey, *The North American Indians in Early Photographs.* New York: Dorset Press, 1986.

Forbes, Jack D., *Native Americans of California and Nevada.* Healdsburg, Calif.: Naturegraph Publishers, 1969.

Gibson, Robert O., *The Chumash.* New York: Chelsea House Publishers, 1991.

Heizer, Robert F., ed.:
California. Vol. 8 in *Handbook of North American Indians.* Washington, D.C.: Smithsonian Institution, 1978.
The Destruction of California Indians: A Collection of Documents from the Period 1847 to 1865 in Which Are Described Some of the Things That Happened to Some of the Indians of California. Lincoln: University of Nebraska Press, 1993.

Heizer, Robert F., and Alan J. Almquist, *The Other Californians: Prejudice and Discrimination under Spain, Mexico, and the United States to 1920.* Berkeley: University of California Press, 1971.

Heizer, Robert F., and Albert B. Elsasser, *The Natural World of the California Indians* (California Natural History Guides no. 46). Berkeley: University of California Press, 1980.

Heizer, Robert F., and Theodora Kroeber, eds., *Ishi the Last Yahi: A Documentary History.* Berkeley: University of California Press, 1979.

Heizer, R. F., and M. A. Whipple, eds., *The California Indians: A Source Book.* Berkeley: University of California Press, 1971.

Heth, Charlotte, ed., *Native American Dance: Ceremonies and Social Traditions.* Washington, D.C.: Smithsonian Institution, 1992.

Hewes, Minna, and Gordon Hewes, eds. and trans., *Indian Life and Customs at Mission San Luis Rey: A Record of California Mission Life by Pablo Tac.* San Luis Rey, Calif.: Old Mission San Luis Rey, 1958.

Hill, Jane H., and Rosinda Nolasquez, eds., *Mulu' wetam: The First People—Cupeño Oral History and Language.* Banning, Calif.: Malki Museum Press, 1973.

Hurtado, Albert L., *Indian Survival on the California Frontier.* New Haven: Yale University Press, 1988.

Hutchinson, C. Alan, *Frontier Settlement in Mexican California: The Híjar-Padrés Colony, and Its Origins, 1769-1835.* New Haven: Yale University Press, 1969.

James, George Wharton, *In and Out of the Old Missions of California: An Historical and Pictorial Account of the Franciscan Missions.* Boston: Little, Brown, 1927.

Keyworth, C. L., *California Indians.* New York: Facts On File, 1991.

Kroeber, A. L.:
Handbook of the Indians of California. Vol. 1. St. Clair Shores, Mich.: Scholarly Press, 1972 (reprint of 1925 edition).
Handbook of the Indians of California. New York: Dover Publications, 1976.

Kroeber, Theodora, *Ishi in Two Worlds: A Biography of the Last Wild Indian in North America.* Berkeley: University of California Press, 1961.

Librado, Fernando, *Breath of the Sun: Life in Early California As Told by a Chumash Indian, Fernando Librado to John P. Harrington.* Ed. by Travis Hudson. Banning, Calif.: Malki Museum Press, 1980.

Margolin, Malcolm, *The Ohlone Way: Indian Life in the San Francisco-Monterey Bay Area.* Berkeley: Heyday Books, 1978.

Margolin, Malcolm, ed., *The Way We Lived: California Indian Reminiscences, Stories, and Songs.* Berkeley: Heyday Books, 1981.

Mathes, Valerie Sherer, *Helen Hunt Jackson and Her Indian Reform Legacy.* Austin: University of Texas Press, 1990.

Moratto, Michael J., *California Archaeology.* Orlando: Academic Press, 1984.

Morgado, Martin J., *Junípero Serra: A Pictorial Biography.* Monterey, Calif.: Siempre Adelante Publishing, 1991.

Moser, Christopher L.:
American Indian Basketry of Northern California. Riverside, Calif.: Riverside Museum Press, 1989.
Native American Basketry of Central California. Riverside, Calif.: Riverside Museum Press, 1986.
Native American Basketry of Southern California. Riverside, Calif.: Riverside Museum Press, 1993.

Nabokov, Peter, ed., *Native American Testimony: A Chronicle of Indian-White Relations from Prophecy to the Present, 1492-1992.* New York: Viking Penguin, 1991.

Neuerburg, Norman, *The Decoration of the California Missions.* Santa Barbara, Calif.: Bellerophon Books, 1989.

Norton, Jack, *When Our Worlds Cried: Genocide in Northwestern California.* San Francisco: Indian Historian Press, 1979.

Ortiz, Bev, *It Will Live Forever: Traditional Yosemite Indian Acorn Preparation.* Berkeley: Heyday Books, 1991.

Phillips, George Harwood:
Chiefs and Challengers: Indian Resistance and Cooperation in Southern California. Berkeley: University of California Press, 1975.
The Enduring Struggle: Indians in California History. San Francisco: Boyd & Fraser Publishing, 1981.
Indians and Intruders in Central California, 1769-1849. Norman: University of Oklahoma Press, 1993.

Powers, Stephen, *Tribes of California.* Berkeley: University of California Press, 1976.

Rawls, James J., *Indians of California: The Changing Image.* Norman: University of Oklahoma Press, 1986.

Shipek, Florence Connolly:
Delfina Cuero: Her Autobiography–An Account of Her Last Years and Her Ethnobotanic Contributions. Menlo Park, Calif.: Ballena Press, 1991.
Pushed into the Rocks: Southern California Indian Land Tenure, 1769-1986. Lincoln: University of Nebraska Press, 1988.

Sunset Editors, *The California Missions: A Pictorial History.* Menlo Park, Calif.: Sunset Publishing, 1991.

Thomas, David Hurst, ed., *Archaeological and Historical Perspectives on the Spanish Borderlands West.* Vol. 1 of *Columbian Consequences.* Washington, D.C.: Smithsonian Institution Press, 1989.

Thompson, Lucy, *To the American Indian: Reminiscences of a Yurok Woman.* Berkeley: Heyday Books, 1991.

Trenton, Patricia, and Patrick T. Houlihan, *Native Americans: Five Centuries of Changing Images.* New York: Harry N. Abrams, 1989.

Warburton, Austen D., and Joseph F. Endert, *Indian Lore of the North California Coast.* Santa Clara, Calif.: Pacific Pueblo Press, 1966.

Webb, Edith Buckland, *Indian Life at the Old Missions.* Lincoln: University of Nebraska Press, 1982.

Weber, David J., *The Mexican Frontier, 1821-1846.* Albuquerque: University of New Mexico Press, 1982.

Weber, Francis J., ed., *El Caminito Real: A Documentary History of California's Asistencias.* Hong Kong: Yee Tin Tong Printing Press, 1988.

PERIODICALS

Alvarez, Susan H., and David W. Peri, "Acorns: The Staff of Life." *News from Native California,* September/October 1987.

Anderson, M. Kat:
"California Indian Horticulture." *Fremontia,* Vol. 18, no. 2, 1990.
"The Mountains Smell like Fire." *Fremontia,* Vol. 21, no. 4, 1993.

Anderson, Kat, and Gary Paul Nabhan, "Gardeners in Eden." *Wilderness,* Fall 1991.

Davis, Lee, "Locating the Live Museum." *News from Native California,* Fall 1989.

Forbes, Jack D., "The Native American Experience in California History." *California Historical Quarterly,* September 1971.

Franco, Hector, "That Place Needs a Good Fire." *News from Native California,* Spring 1993.

Hurtado, Albert L., "Sexuality in California's Franciscan Missions: Cultural Perceptions and Sad Realities." *California History,* Fall 1992.

Lummis, Charles, "The Exiles of Cupa." *Out West,* Vol. 16, no. 5, 1902.

Margolin, Malcolm, and Jeannine Gendar, eds., "California Indians and the Environment" (Special Reports no. 1), *News from Native California,* Spring 1992.

Neuerberg, Norman, "Painting in the California Missions." *American Art Review,* July 1977.

Ortiz, Bev, "It Will Live Forever: Yosemite Indian Acorn Preparation." *News from Native California,* November/December 1988.

Peri, David W., "Plant of the Season: Oaks." *News from Native California,* November/December 1987.

Phillips, George Harwood, "Indians in Los Angeles, 1781-1875: Economic Integration, Social Disintegration." *Pacific Historical Review,* August 1980.

Rojas, Arnold, "Who Were the Vaqueros?" *The Californians,* November/December 1992.

Thompson, Lucy, "Reminiscences of a Yurok Aristocrat." *The Californians,* November/December 1992.

Wallace, Grant, "The Exiles of Cupa." *Out West,* Vol. 19, no. I, 1903.

OTHER PUBLICATIONS

Anderson, Marion Kathleen, "The Experimental Approach to Assessment of the Potential Ecological Effects of Horticultural Practices by Indigenous Peoples on California Wildlands." Doctoral dissertation. Berkeley: University of California, 1993.

Brandes, Ray, trans., "The Costansó Narrative of the Portolá Expedition: First Chronicle of the Spanish Conquest of Alta California." A Facsimile reproduction of the original copy in the Los Angeles Public Library.

Brumbaugh, Lee, "Paradise and Survival: Ceremonial Indian Dance in Northern California, 1988-1992." Berkeley: Phoebe A. Hearst Museum of Anthropology, 1992.

Davis, Lee, "On This Earth: Hupa Land Domains, Images, and Ecology on 'Deddeh Ninnisan.'" Doctoral dissertation. Berkeley: University of California, 1988.

"Native American Art in the Denver Art Museum." Denver: Denver Art Museum, 1979.

Theodoratus Cultural Research, "Ethnographic Inventory for Public Law 95-341: North Central California." Fair Oaks, Calif.: April 1984.

PICTURE CREDITS

pal Museum, A8-95, Harwood Hall Collection, photo by Chris L. Moser—San Diego Historical Society, E. H. Davis Collection. **73:** NAA, Smithsonian Institution, Washington, D.C., neg. no. 75-16219—courtesy The Oakland Museum History Department (3). **74, 75:** NAA, Smithsonian Institution, Washington, D.C., neg. no. 75-14715; courtesy The Oakland Museum History Department (3); Kunstkamera, St. Petersburg Museum of Anthropology and Ethnography and European House Publishers, St. Petersburg, Russia—NAA, Smithsonian Institution, Washington, D.C., neg. no. 47,750-B. **76:** San Diego Historical Society, E. H. Davis Collection; courtesy The Oakland Museum History Department (2). **77:** Courtesy The Oakland Museum History Department, except middle, NAA, Smithsonian Institution, Washington, D.C., neg. no. 41,887-L. **78:** Courtesy The Oakland Museum History Department—San Diego Historical Society, E. H. Davis Collection—Ulster Museum, Belfast, Northern Ireland. **79:** Courtesy The Oakland Museum History Department—Field Museum of Natural History, Chicago, neg. no. A9518—Riverside Municipal Museum, A8-108, Harwood Hall Collection, photo by Chris L. Moser. **80:** Courtesy The Oakland Museum History Department (2); courtesy The Bancroft Library, University of California at Berkeley. **81:** Ulster Museum, Belfast, Northern Ireland—courtesy The Oakland Museum History Department; NAA, Smithsonian Institution, Washington, D.C., neg. no. 76-16271—Riverside Municipal Museum, A671-35, Harwood Mitchell Collection, photo by Chris L. Moser. **82:** Phoebe A. Hearst Museum of Anthropology, University of California at Berkeley; Riverside Municipal Museum, A1-218, Cornelius E. Rumsey Collection, photo by Chris L. Moser—courtesy Southwest Museum, Los Angeles, photo no. CT.294. **83:** Courtesy The Oakland Museum History Department; collection of Palm Springs Desert Museum, PSDM no. 506-74A, photo by Chris L. Moser—photo by Carmelo Guadagno, courtesy National Museum of the American Indian, Smithsonian Institution, cat. no. 21/4783. **84:** Copyright British Museum, London—The Huntington Library, San Marino, California. **86, 87:** Southwest Museum, Los Angeles,

drawing 22.G.978Q. **88:** Library of Congress. **89:** Gianni Dagli Orti, Paris. **90, 91:** Courtesy The Bancroft Library, University of California at Berkeley. **92:** Map by Maryland CartoGraphics, Inc. **94, 95:** The Fine Arts Museums of San Francisco, gift of Eleanor Martin, acc. no. 37573. **97:** Museo Naval, Madrid. **99:** San Diego Historical Society, E. H. Davis Collection; Henry Groskinsky, courtesy Mission San Carlos de Borromeo. **100, 101:** From *The Missions of California* by Stanley Young, photos by Melba Levick © 1988, published by Chronicle Books—William B. Dewey, courtesy Mission Santa Ines; William B. Dewey, courtesy Mission San Gabriel. **103:** Lompoc Valley Historical Society, Inc. **104:** Drawing by Pablo Tac from *Indian Life at Mission San Luis Rey* ed. and trans. by M. and G. Hewes, Old Mission San Luis Rey, California, 1958—San Diego Historical Society, photograph collection. **107:** Constance Du Bois Collection, San Diego Museum of Man—San Diego Historical Society, E. H. Davis Collection. **108:** San Diego Museum of Man—San Diego Historical Society, E. H. Davis Collection. **109:** Edward H. Davis photo, Constance Du Bois Collection, San Diego Museum of Man—San Diego Museum of Man. **110:** San Diego Historical Society, E. H. Davis Collection. **111:** The Huntington Library, San Marino, California—Edward H. Davis photo, Constance Du Bois Collection, San Diego Museum of Man. **113:** Courtesy National Museum of the American Indian, Smithsonian Institution, photo no. 24371. **114, 115:** Santa Barbara Museum of Natural History, Dovida Treiman, photographer. **116, 117:** The Huntington Library, San Marino, California—Henry Groskinsky, courtesy Old Mission Santa Ines. **118, 119:** Courtesy The Bancroft Library, University of California at Berkeley. **121:** Phoebe A. Hearst Museum of Anthropology, University of California at Berkeley. **122:** Courtesy Southwest Museum, Los Angeles, nos. LS.5825—LS.5821. **124, 125:** Courtesy The Bancroft Library, University of California at Berkeley. **126, 127:** Library of Congress. **128, 129:** Background and top left Library of Congress; courtesy Southwest Museum, Los Angeles, photo nos. N.19837; P.2043. **130, 131:** Inset Library of Congress—courtesy South-

west Museum, Los Angeles, photo no. N.22470. **132, 133:** Background San Diego Historical Society, E. H. Davis Collection; insets courtesy Southwest Museum, Los Angeles, photo nos. P.1404; P.1407. **134, 135:** Courtesy Southwest Museum, Los Angeles, photo no. N.40000. **136:** Courtesy Southwest Museum, Los Angeles, photo no. N.24675. **138:** Map by Maryland CartoGraphics, Inc. **140, 141:** The Huntington Library, San Marino, California. **143:** Courtesy The Bancroft Library, University of California at Berkeley. **145, 146:** Phoebe A. Hearst Museum of Anthropology, University of California at Berkeley. **147:** California State Indian Museum, photo by Nikki Pahl—Phoebe A. Hearst Museum of Anthropology, University of California at Berkeley (2)—California State Indian Museum, photo by Nikki Pahl. **148:** Phoebe A. Hearst Museum of Anthropology, University of California at Berkeley. **150:** Courtesy University of Virginia. **152, 153:** Mendocino County Historical Society, Robert J. Lee Collection. **154:** Courtesy Peter E. Palmquist. **156, 157:** NAA, Smithsonian Institution, Washington, D.C., neg. no. 2854-E. **158, 159:** © Carr Clifton—courtesy The Bancroft Library, University of California at Berkeley. **160, 161:** The Huntington Library, San Marino, California—NAA, Smithsonian Institution, Washington, D.C., neg. no. 3054-A. **162, 163:** NAA, Smithsonian Institution, Washington, D.C., neg. no. 3052; Phoebe A. Hearst Museum of Anthropology, University of California at Berkeley. **165:** Courtesy Peter E. Palmquist. **166:** Constance Du Bois photo, San Diego Museum of Man—Ned Gillette photo, Constance Du Bois Collection, San Diego Museum of Man. **167:** Constance Du Bois photos, San Diego Museum of Man. **168:** S. M. Brosins photos, Constance Du Bois Collection, San Diego Museum of Man. **169:** Constance Du Bois photos, San Diego Museum of Man (2)—S. M. Brosins photo, Constance Du Bois Collection, San Diego Museum of Man. **172, 173:** Courtesy Peter E. Palmquist. **174, 175:** Courtesy Juanita F. Montes; Palm Springs Historical Society, neg. no. 88-04-131. **176, 177:** © 1969 Alan Copeland/Black Star. **179-185:** Background courtesy The Oakland Museum History Department, insets by Lee Brumbaugh.

INDEX